C000067435

ISLAND KITCHEN

Illustrations on front cover and overleaf from paintings by Jean de Garis

ISLAND KITCHEN

A *Book* of *Seasonal* *Cookery* from the *Channel* *Islands*

Marguerite Paul

(author of *Channel Fish*)

SEAFLOWER BOOKS

Published in 2003
Reprinted in 2004, 2008 and 2012 by
SEAFLOWER BOOKS
11 Regents Place
Bradford on Avon   Wiltshire   BA15 1ED

www. ex-librisbooks.co.uk

Design and typesetting by
Seaflower Books

Printed in Britain by
Martins The Printers
Berwick Upon Tweed
Northumberland   TD15 1RS

ISBN 1 903341 18 3

Acknowledgements

My sincere thanks to our dear friends Owen and Fiona Le Tissier who must surely know how much we value their ongoing friendship! And to many people and organisations for their support, help and encouragement in the preparation of this book during the last two years or so. In particular, I would like to mention:

In Jersey: Nan du Feu, for the many anecdotes of her early life in Jersey as well as the Jersey patois; the late Eileen Le Sueur, a well known Jersey lady who kindly invited us to her home, and who, over delicious tea and cake, told us heartwarming stories and provided valuable personal recipes; The Jersey Island Federation of Women's Institutes for permission to quote from their charming booklet *Buoun Appétit*; Mrs Angela Underwood of La Société Jersiaise.

In Guernsey: Bob Gill for proof reading the Guernsey patois; David Le Conte, President of La Société Guernesiaise, for permission to quote from Marie de Garis' book on Guernsey Folklore; Bill Gallienne, also of La Société Guernesiaise, for proof reading historical references; Dr Daryl Ogier, Guernsey States Archives Service, for local historical information; Dr Gregory Stevens-Cox for permission to quote from his late father's booklet *Guernsey Dishes of Bygone Days*; June Bright for carefully testing various recipes; Jean de Garis for permission to reproduce her lovely paintings of an Island Kitchen on the front cover and frontispiece; Jason Hamon at the Forest Stores for advice as well as meat for various recipes; finally, my husband, willing guinea pig and stickler for Plain English !

CONTENTS

SPRING

Wild Food

Fish

Meat

Poultry

Vegetables

Wild Food

Fruit

Milk – Our Golden Liquor

Wedding Breakfast Baking

Easter

SUMMER

Vegetables

Fish

Barbecues

AUTUMN

Meat

Fish

Vegetables

Fruit

Chutneys, Pickles, Jellies, Jams & Beverages

WINTER

Meat

Poultry

Fish

Vegetables

Desserts

Conserves

Introduction

A few years ago, my daughter astounded me when she declined the offer, from a boyfriend, of a live crab that he had just caught and which he probably considered to be a gift showing his high esteem! She rejected the crab, saying she would not know what to do with it. The incident prompted me to put together *Channel Fish*, a cookery book dealing with all aspects of the fish found in these waters.

More recently, a pleasant dinner at friends, where we enjoyed nettle soup and, later in the meal, wild spinach, started me thinking about just what local produce is still available in our small islands. We are all aware of concerns over genetically modified crops, food miles and sustainability. At the same time, interest in organic production, farmers' markets, seasonal eating and the growing Slow Food movement – all point to a yearning for a return to traditional fare. The situation in the wider world is one thing, but what is the current status of our own gastronomic heritage when it comes to trying to eat *à l'ancienne*?

Thinking cap thus firmly on, my ensuing investigations into the history of our local produce soon made me realise that I was mining a narrow seam. It became clear that, unavoidably, in islands as small as ours, we have, since the earliest times, depended on a wide range of imports to provide the variety in eating – and everything else – that humans crave. The geographical location of the islands led inevitably to a seafaring tradition which encouraged the movement of goods. Indeed, you could say that world trade had been invented right here in the Channel Islands!

Today, not even those very basic Channel Islands' recipes - bean jar or croc and *gâche mêlaïe* can readily be made using entirely local produce for, in the islands, few pigs are now raised and no local wheat is milled into flour.

Nevertheless, my enquiries led me to discover that a surprisingly wide range of truly local produce does still exist. For example, fruit and vegetables, not forgetting the 'hedge veg' – a means by which enthusiastic gardeners can sell their produce generally from a box 'on the hedge' and where an honesty tin, or even a jam jar, collects the amount due! Also dairy products, fish, meat, poultry, eggs, *charcuterie* – even cider – are all available. If you are prepared to make the effort, it is still possible to obtain and enjoy the benefits of truly local resources – including some organic ones – to the full.

Finally, many of the recipes in this book are Channel Island favourites or are based upon them, while others I have put together myself. They are intended to promote locally produced 'basics' but, of course, do include many imported foods. My recipes are unsophisticated as they are intended for everyday use and I have tried to minimise the list of ingredients. At the same time, I hope that readers will be reminded of times past and that they will continue to use many of those recipes handed down as well as trying others I have included. Island produce is our heritage and how we use it part of our culture.

Marguerite Paul
Guernsey, 2003

Some History

From antiquity, the Channel Islands, although nominally forming part of the Duchy of Normandy, had always been fiercely independent. In 1066, the conquest of England by William Duke of Normandy made little difference locally and it was not until the subsequent loss of Normandy by the English King John in 1204 that the powerful local Seigneurs had to choose whether to continue to owe allegiance to the French King or to align themselves with the English Sovereign. As many of these Seigneurs had large land holdings in England they decided to remain loyal to King John. Of course, the local people were never consulted! However, although the Channel Islands thenceforth 'belonged' to England, the original Norman ties remained strong. Appreciating this and to ensure the continuing loyalty of his island subjects, in 1213 King John granted various privileges to the islands including exemption from Crown taxes and Customs duties. This was a green light for those tough seafaring people; both smuggling and later privateering played important roles in the islands' economic development. It has been said that St Peter Port's distinctive skyline is at least partly due to the rewards of privateering during the sixteenth and seventeenth centuries.

By the early 1700s the islands had become well known as an *entrepôt* for goods from elsewhere which could then enter England, free of duty. This *entrepôt* trade also encouraged the export of surplus local produce such as woollen goods, cattle, fish and cider. Over time, the Islands have become justifiably famous for a succession of exports. For example: the eponymous Jersey and Guernsey woollen garments, Guernsey and Jersey 'toms', the Jersey Royal potato, (profiting from the islands' favourable geography, warmed by the Gulf Stream) and, above all, the two distinctive Channel Islands cattle breeds, renowned throughout the world for their high butterfat yield, the result of successful selective breeding from Norman and Breton stock, helped by the isolation of island environments.

Let's Start…

As mentioned in my Introduction, interest in a return to seasonal eating habits must surely underlie our efforts to recreate the 'good old days'. Who has not been seduced by the exotic contents of the supermarket deep freezers? But can anything from the deep freeze truly equal the simple pleasure – and goodness of, say, a blackberry freshly picked from our hedgerows?

Thus I have arranged the recipes in this book in order of seasonal availability… and where better start than with Spring?

SPRING

Jersey French	*ernouvé* (m), *printemps* (m), *r'vèrdie*
Guernsey French	*lé r'nouvé* (m)

March ~ April ~ May

Wordsworth sums up Spring better than anyone else with his 'host of golden daffodils'. Those first glimpses of a daffodil in a field or a primrose in a hedgerow are welcome signs that the 'dead' season of winter will soon be ending to be replaced by the happy, burgeoning, annual renewal – truly, the sap is rising, as the saying goes.

Astronomically, Spring begins at the March equinox, i.e., 21st March, but my impatience leads me to think of the first of the month as the beginning of Spring! However, it is still too early in the cycle for spring garden produce for the table and fruits, of course, are even further away.

Nevertheless, things are stirring and on walks in the country you will be able to collect nettles and sorrel while, by the sea-shore, wild spinach (also known as sea beet) with its shiny, dark green leaves, simply oozing good health, will be very much in evidence.

Easter is on the horizon, preceded by Pancake Day and Lent. Mothering Sunday is a mid-Lent pause for celebration. It is also an occasion for baking and enjoying Simnel Cake, a marzipan covered delight flavoured with saffron. Many still fast during Lent and abstain from meat on Good Friday. Secretly, weight watchers probably welcome the Lenten fast for mortal reasons.

In Jersey, *gâche à fouée* was baked. These fairly thick, flat discs of bread were eaten with butter. Another Jersey custom was *des fliottes*. These small buns or dumplings were cooked in boiling milk and served with some of the milk poured over and sprinkled with sugar.

Superstition has it that cakes and buns cooked on Good Friday never go mouldy!

Good Friday was also a day of almsgiving in the form of bread and cake.

Easter – a time for rejoicing. We don't pay as much attention to bringing out the 'Sunday Best' and Easter Bonnets but children still go round asking for eggs. Often they were wrapped individually in a cloth and boiled with onion skins until hard and then cooled in the water. Unwrapping them would reveal marbled eggs when a little polishing with a dab of grease produced a lovely golden egg. Now, more often than not, the real one has given way to the chocolate eggs of today!

So, with Spring in the air, I suggest a walk in the countryside.

Spinach

| Jersey French | sea beet | *bette* (f) |
| Guernsey French | sea beet | *baette* or *bette dé bànque* (f) |

Wild spinach or sea beet is found throughout the islands, mainly in country lanes or along the sea-shore. It tends to be a low-growing plant with shiny leaves and can become quite bushy.

Spinach Moulds

Serves 4
250g/8oz wild sea beet or 1 bundle of fresh spinach
2 eggs
275ml/10fl oz double cream
Grated nutmeg
Salt and pepper

Remove the stalks and wash the spinach. Cook, then thoroughly squeeze dry.
Whizz the spinach in the food processor. Add the eggs and cream. Season, adding a little grated nutmeg.
Pour the mixture into buttered moulds. Cover with foil and cook in a roasting tin, half filled with water for about thirty minutes, 190°C, 375°F, Gas 5, until set. If they seem a bit wobbly, cook for a further five to ten minutes.
Leave to relax for about fifteen minutes before running a knife around and turning them out.
Serve with tomato or hollandaise sauce swirled around.

W
I
L
D

F
O
O
D

Cream of Spinach Soup

Serves 4

375g/12oz wild sea beet or 1 bundle of spinach
30g/1oz butter
1 medium onion   425ml/15fl oz milk
1 clove garlic   4 tbsp double cream
30g/1oz plain flour   Nutmeg
425ml/15fl oz chicken or vegetable stock   Salt and pepper

This soup is quickly made as overcooking makes it dull in colour.

Fry the chopped onion and garlic in the butter for about five minutes. Add the roughly chopped spinach, stock and seasoning. Bring to the boil and cook for five minutes until the spinach has collapsed. Whizz in the food processor and return to the saucepan.

Mix the flour to a creamy paste with a little of the milk. Stir into the soup, add the remaining milk bringing slowly to the boil, stirring all the time.

Remove from the heat, stir in the cream and a little grated nutmeg. Serve.

Pancakes stuffed with Spinach

Serves 4

Pancake batter
60g/2oz plain flour   1 tbsp curry paste
1 egg   Salt and pepper
150ml/5fl oz milk
30g/1oz melted butter   Sauce
Salt and pepper   30g/1oz butter
                                        30g/1oz flour
Filling   275ml/10fl oz milk
375g/12oz wild sea beet or   100g/3oz grated cheese,
1 bundle fresh spinach   e.g. cheddar
250g/8oz cream cheese   Salt and pepper

Make the pancakes by beating the egg in a bowl. Stir in the flour, melted butter and milk. Whisk until smooth, season with salt and pepper. Alternatively, whizz all the ingredients in the food processor. Make eight pancakes, piling them on a plate as you go; a 20cms/8inch pan is a good size to use.

Cook the spinach. Drain, squeezing out as much water as possible.

Roughly chop the spinach and put in a bowl. Stir in the curry paste and cream cheese. Season. Share the mixture between the eight pancakes. Roll each and place in an oblong ovenproof dish.

To make the sauce: melt the butter, add the flour stirring until smooth. Gradually add the milk, stirring to keep the sauce smooth. Add the cheese, reserving a little. Bring to the boil, season and pour over the pancakes. Sprinkle with the reserved cheese.

Bake in a moderate oven 375°F, 190°C, Gas 5 for about twenty minutes.

Spinach Pie or Quiche

Serves 4 to 6
20-23cms/8-9inch flan dish

Pastry Case
150g/5oz plain flour   4 tbsp cold water
120g/4oz butter   Pinch salt

Filling
375g wild sea beet or 1 bundle spinach
3 spring onions   150 ml/5fl oz cream
1 tbsp chopped parsley   60g/2oz grated cheddar cheese
3 eggs   Salt and pepper

Make the pastry by putting the flour and salt in a bowl. Grate in the butter and mix to a stiff dough with the water. Alternatively use a food processor. Line the flan dish.
Cook the spinach until it collapses. Drain and squeeze out as much water as possible. Chop it and scatter over the pastry with the finely sliced spring onion on top. In a bowl beat the eggs, stir in the cream and parsley. Season. Pour over the spinach. Sprinkle with the cheese. Bake for thirty to forty minutes at 190°C, 375°F, Gas 5.

Nettles

Jersey French	*ortchies* (f)
Guernsey French	*ortie* (f)

Nettles are found everywhere and are a plant that children very quickly learn to recognise and give a wide birth! But they do have an up-side. They are full of iron, formic acid and natural histamine. They improve blood circulation and purify the system.

I learnt from the Jersey W.I. booklet *Buoun Appetit* that an infusion or tea made with nettles is good for curing pleurisy; it purifies the blood, opens pipes and passages to the lungs thus easing breathing and loosenlng tough phlegm, heals a sore throat, kills gravel and stones and many other complaints which are too numerous to list.

In addition to their health benefits, nettles also taste very good so, armed with gloves, a pair of scissors and a bucket, I snipped the young shoots from the top of the plants.

Nettle Soup

Serves 4
90g/3oz nettle leaves
1 onion
1 carrot
1 clove garlic
1 medium potato

800ml/1.5 pints stock
2 tbsp double cream
30g/1oz butter
Salt and pepper

Chop the onions, carrot, potato and garlic and fry in the butter for five minutes.
Add the stock, nettles and seasoning. Simmer for twenty minutes.
Strain the soup. Whizz the nettles and vegetables in the food processor adding a ladle of stock to get it going.
Rinse the pan. Add the puréed vegetables and stock. Just before serving, gently heat to boiling point. Remove from the heat, add the cream.
Serve with a bowl of garlicked croûtons.

Sorrel

| Jersey French | *suthelle* (f) |
| Guernsey French | *surelle* (f) |

Wild sorrel is found in the fields and hedgerows as early as January. Its spear-shaped leaves taste sour, almost vinegary, but at the same time add a lemony zing to soups, sauces, salads and mayonnaise. Sorrel is easily grown but the seed to use is the French sorrel: *Rumex Scutatus*.

Care must be taken not to overcook sorrel as it loses its colour and very quickly collapses. Avoid using uncoated aluminium saucepans as the acid in the sorrel may react with the metal.

Sorrel Soup

Serves 4
Approximately 30-35 sorrel leaves
2 carrots
2 sticks celery
1 leek
1 small onion
60g/2oz butter
3 tbsp double cream
550ml/20fl oz chicken or vegetable stock
Salt and pepper

In a pan, melt the butter, add the chopped onion, leek, celery and carrots. Season and cook for about five minutes, occasionally stirring. Add the stock and cook for twenty-five minutes, add the sliced sorrel and cook for five minutes. Cool, then whizz in the food processor. When ready to serve, bring slowly to the boil, remove from the heat, stir in the cream. Serve with a bowl of croûtons.

WILD FOOD

Sorrel Mayonnaise

To make approximately 150ml/5fl oz
2 egg yolks
1 good tsp french mustard
1 tbsp wine vinegar
150ml/5fl oz olive oil
Salt and pepper
6 sorrel leaves - dandelion leaves can be used

Place the egg yolks in the food processor. Add the mustard and vinegar. Start whizzing, very gradually adding the olive oil until thick and creamy. Season.

Roll the sorrel leaves into a cigar shape, finely slice. Add to the mayonnaise. A quick whizz and it is ready.

Serve in a bowl with any fish or shellfish.

Sorrel with Potato Salad

Serves 4
1 kg/2lbs potatoes
1 small onion
3-4 rashers unsmoked streaky bacon
1 hard boiled egg
Approximately 8 sorrel leaves
2 tbsp chopped parsley
6 tbsp olive oil
Salt and pepper

Boil the potatoes. While they are cooking, fry the sliced onion and streaky bacon in two tbsp olive oil. Put to one side.

In a bowl, slice the hot potatoes. Roll the sorrel leaves into a cigar shape, slice and add to the hot potatoes. Gently turn. Season, adding the remaining oil. Garnish with the onion, bacon, chopped hard boiled egg and chopped parsley, turning all of it before serving.

Scallops

Jersey French   *couinne* (f), *pitonne* (f), *scallope* (f), *vanné* (m)
Guernsey French   *vannet* (m), *vaunet d'maïr* (m)

Scallop beds around the islands remained undisturbed for hundreds of years simply because there was no way of fishing these molluscs. Divers hadn't arrived on the scene and methods of fishing hadn't created nets that could retrieve fish and shellfish living on the seabed. Along with the diver and new ways of fishing, these rich beds were soon overfished. Fortunately, protection laws have been introduced and as a result numbers are increasing.

The Great or smaller Queen are the two main edible ones found locally.

When buying loose scallops, ask your fishmonger for assurance that they are really fresh as this is one shellfish that can be opened and displayed without its shell.

Scallops with Cider

Serves 4
3 or 4 scallops including the
  coral per person
220ml/8fl oz dry cider
  (about half a 440ml can)
150ml/5fl oz fish stock
3 tbsp cream

60g/2oz butter
3 shallots
Half a lemon
1 tbsp chopped chives or parsley
Salt and pepper

Marinate the scallops in the cider, lemon juice and seasoning for about one hour.

Once marinated, pour the marinade into a pan with the fish stock and chopped shallots, simmer for about ten minutes. Add the scallops to the pan and poach for four minutes, no longer. Remove with a slotted spoon and keep warm. Reduce the liquid until thickish. Remove from the heat and stir in the cream.

Beat in the butter, piece by piece, until you have a thick glossy sauce. Stir in the chives or parsley, reserving a little for garnishing. Place the scallops on plates. Reheat the sauce, pour over and around. Garnish with the remaining chives or parsley.

F
I
S
H

Scallops with Blinis

Serves 4

Blinis

180g/6oz plain flour or 120g/4oz plain
  flour and 60g/2oz buckwheat flour
1 egg
150ml/5fl oz warm milk
60g/2oz melted butter & a little for
  greasing the pan

1 tbsp sour cream
1 tsp dried yeast
Quarter tsp sugar
Quarter tsp salt
2 tbsp warm water

Put the warm water in a bowl, add the sugar and sprinkle over the yeast. Leave for five minutes to bubble.

Place the salt and flour in a roomy bowl. In a smaller bowl, mix the egg, sour cream and melted butter. Pour into the flour and mix with a wooden spoon adding the milk a little at a time until you have a thick batter. Place the bowl in a plastic bag and leave in a warm place for one hour to prove.

Take a griddle or non stick frying pan. Brush with melted butter. Gradually pour in a tablespoonful of batter, coaxing it into a blini about 7cms/3inches wide. Cook about two minutes on each side. Keep warm in a tea towel until needed.

12 scallops with the coral
2 cloves garlic
Approximately 6 sage leaves
1 tbsp capers
2 tbsp calvados

Juice of half a lemon
3 spring onions
1 tbsp chopped parsley
60g/2oz butter

In a roomy pan, fry the scallops in the butter. Add the chopped sage leaves, spring onions and garlic. Cook for two minutes, turn and cook the other side. Add the calvados, lemon juice, parsley and capers. Place three scallops on each plate, place two blinis alongside. Pour the buttery juice from the pan over the scallops.

Mussels

Jersey French	*moûle* (f), *chuchette* (f), *becque-dé-corbin* (f), *orté dé geniche* (m)
Guernsey French	*moule* (f)

Spring is a good time for mussels even though they are available all year round.

Try not to store mussels but, if you have to, keep them in a cool place covered with a wet piece of sacking or seaweed. Don't cover them with water or they will suffocate and die. Don't store for more than twenty-four hours.

Most mussels have been scrubbed and the fibrous beard removed. Give them the once over, throwing out any that are open or damaged.

Like the oyster, the mussel can be cooked in many different ways, the favourite must be Moules Marinière but here is a variation.

Mussels with White Wine & Cream

Serve 4

2.5 kilos/5lbs mussels	2 cloves garlic
1 onion or 4 shallots	3 tbsp chopped parsley
2 egg yolks	150ml/5fl oz dry white wine
150ml/5fl oz double cream	Salt and pepper
30g/1oz butter	

In a large saucepan, gently simmer the finely chopped onion and garlic in the wine for ten minutes. Don't add any water as a lot will come from the mussels as they open.

Add the mussels, cover and gently shake the pan for about five minutes until all are open. Tip into a colander, keeping the liquor. Discard any that are unopened.

Rapidly boil the liquor to reduce to about 150ml/5fl oz. Add the cream and slowly bring to the boil. Remove from the heat and whisk in the egg yolks. Divide the butter into small pieces, gradually whisking them into the liquor. Add half the parsley. Season.

Tip the mussels into a large bowl or four bowls. Scatter with the remaining parsley and serve with the creamy wine sauce. It is perfectly acceptable to use the hinged shell of a mussel to extract the meat.

Ormers

Jersey French	*ormèr* (m)
Guernsey French	*ormé* (m) hp, *ormaërs* (m) lp

A seasonal tradition which continues to this day is ormering. With the huge tides of Winter and most of Spring, out come the hooks, wellies and waterproof clothing as hardy hunters brave the wind and cold in search of this elusive mollusc, endlessly turning rocks. If you ask anyone how many they have found, the most usual reply is either 'enough for a feed' or 'not enough for a feed'.

Islanders wax lyrical over the ormer and are prepared to pay extortionate prices for it. Here, I must include an anecdote from Nan du Feu. While living in Southampton, as a very special treat her mother used to send her a kilner jar full of ormer stew by post from Jersey. This shows our love of the ormer and the trouble taken to share this delicacy.

Factors such as overfishing, degradation of habitat and climate change may in some way have caused the decline in numbers of the ormer. As a result, the States of Jersey and the Bailiwick of Guernsey have passed laws protecting the mollusc. It is only legal to gather ormers between 1st January and 30th April and then only on the day of each new or full moon and the two days following. Reports indicate that numbers are increasing.

In my view, although ormers can be fried, the best way to cook them is in a casserole. The traditional way is with onions and bay leaf but bacon and other herbs may be added.

Three good-sized ormers should be enough but it really depends on how many you have and the size of appetites.

Once home with your ormers, the cleaning process begins. Protect your hand with a glove or towel and hold the ormer in it. With a short, sharp knife cut the muscle attaching the ormer to its shell. With a strong bristled brush, scrub the ormer as there is a lot of grit in the frill. Place the rinsed ormer between two cloths and beat with a mallet or rolling pin to help tenderise it. Be gentle, don't pulverise it. Now it is ready for cooking.

Fry the onions in butter, then put them in a casserole. Toss the ormers in flour and put in the casserole with the bay leaf, season with salt and pepper. Cover with water. Cook four to five hours, checking to make sure there is always enough gravy.

A bowl of boiled potatoes is all that is needed to mash in the gravy.

Sheep

Jersey French	*mouton* (m)
Guernsey French	*berbis* (m), *moutaon* (m)

M
E
A
T

Up until about 1700, Jersey had its own native sheep. It was described by Jean Poingdestre in 1682 as being small but with a unique arrangement of horns. It was replaced by a bigger breed and many hundreds of flocks. For a time in all the islands, sheep were the mainstay in livestock as they provided not only meat and leather but more importantly wool which was in great demand during the lucrative knitting years from 1470 until about 1840. With the decline of knitting, there was less demand for wool. During the seventeenth century, change was taking place with cattle becoming the predominant animal. Now very few sheep are seen and most of the lamb we eat is imported.

There is some confusion over what is lamb. Beef is easier to define: veal means meat from a calf while beef comes from more mature animals. The so called spring lamb is killed at four to six months whereas ordinary lamb is the title applied to older animals. We rarely hear the term mutton these days but, when available, it refers to the excellent meat from castrated sheep of between two and four years-old.

Lamb is traditionally eaten at Easter so my first recipe is:

Roast Stuffed Shoulder of Spring Lamb

Serves 6

1 shoulder of lamb	1 lemon
90g/3 oz white breadcrumbs	2 tbsp chopped parsley
1 small onion	2 tbsp chopped walnuts
2 cloves garlic	6/8 chopped dried apricots
30g/1oz butter	1 egg + 1 yolk
1 tbsp flour	Salt and pepper

Remove the bones from the shoulder – a small sharp knife is a great help. You will probably be left with a very messy looking piece of meat but it doesn't matter. Once stuffed and tied up it will look really good.

Use the bones for stock for the gravy by simmering them for a good hour with a handful of mixed herbs.

Make the stuffing by first of all frying the chopped onion and garlic in the butter until soft. Place the breadcrumbs, herbs, chopped walnuts and apricots and grated lemon peel in a bowl. Add the onion and garlic mixture. Beat the egg and yolk together and add to the breadcrumbs along with the juice of half the lemon. If the mixture seems rather dry, add the juice from the other half. Mix until well amalgamated, season with salt and pepper.

Lay the lamb flat, skin side down. Pile the stuffing in the middle and draw the lamb up so that it resembles a ball, press it down gently. Tie it with several pieces of string so that it feels firm and the stuffing can't escape. Turn it over and gently flatten it a little. Roast in a hot oven 215°C, 425°F, Gas 7 for one hour and then reduce the heat for a further hour. When cooked, place the shoulder on a meat plate, cover with foil and allow it to rest and relax for about fifteen minutes. Drain almost all the fat from the roasting pan. Scrape the bits in the roasting pan loose. Mix in one tbsp plain flour then add the stock from the bones, a little at a time, stirring so that there are no lumps – a small whisk does wonders to remove lumps! Check for seasoning. Before serving, cut and remove the string. Cut the lamb into segments, as if you were cutting a cake. Serve the gravy separately. Roasted potatoes, parsnips and carrots would go well. They could be roasted around the shoulder of lamb.

Roast Lamb with Garlic Gravy

Serves 4

1 small shoulder of lamb
2 cloves garlic
2 or 3 sprigs of rosemary
Salt and pepper

Gravy
1 tbsp peeled cloves of garlic
3 tbsp double cream
250ml/8fl oz stock

A shoulder or leg of lamb with slivers of garlic pushed deep inside the flesh and a scattering of rosemary, slowly roasted until it shrinks from the bone, is my favourite way of eating lamb. The shoulder is sweeter than the leg.

Finely chop the cloves of garlic and place them in a pan with the stock, double cream and seasoning. Gently simmer for thirty minutes. For a smoother gravy, sieve the contents of the pan. For added richness, drain the fat from the joint then tip the remaining juices in the gravy.

Casseroled Lamb Kidneys

Serves 4

12 kidneys
6 slices streaky bacon
30g/1oz butter
2 tbsp flour

1 onion
150ml/5fl oz red wine
A scattering of fresh thyme and rosemary
Salt and pepper

Cut the kidneys in half removing the thick white core. Rinse, pat dry, roll in the flour and fry in butter. Put in an ovenproof casserole. Fry the chopped bacon and onion. Add to the kidneys. Pour over the red wine and add the herbs. Season.

Cook at 190°C, 375°F, Gas 5 for about two hours. Check to make sure it does not dry out.

M
E
A
T

M
E
A
T

Casseroled Lamb Shanks

Serves 4

4 lamb shanks	2 carrots
2 tbsp oil	2-3 bay leaves
1 tin chopped tomatoes	2-3 sprigs rosemary
1 large onion	Salt and pepper

Fry the shanks in the oil until browned all over. Place in a roomy casserole.

Fry the sliced onion and scatter over the shanks. Add the tomatoes, diced carrots, sprigs of rosemary, bay leaves and enough water to just cover them. Season.

Cook in a moderate oven 190°C, 375°F, Gas 5 for about three hours. Check during cooking that there is plenty of liquid.

Serve with roasted potatoes, parsnips and carrots.

~

Goat

| Jersey French | *biche* (f) |
| Guernsey French | *bichaon* (m), *biche* (f), *bichot* (m) |

In the past, goats, like sheep, were numerous in the islands. Goats, unlike sheep, had the added advantage that they could be kept tethered. They were kept for milk and meat. Nan du Feu tells me that, on their farm in Jersey, a goat was kept among the cows in the stable as it was considered it kept them healthy.

Guernsey has its own breed, the Golden Guernsey. A small, pretty animal with a golden coat. Its placid temperament made it popular as a family animal. It was first referred to in a guide book published in 1826 with registration starting in the Guernsey Goat Society's general herd book in 1922. A section for the Golden Guernsey was included by the Society in 1965 as the goats were breeding true to type. The Golden Guernsey Goat Association was formed in 1972, the object being to retain the purity of this unique breed. Sadly, the breed is on the decline but it mustn't be allowed to disappear.

I was fascinated by the story my Aunt Marguerite told me about goats. Her Mother (my Grandmother) was obviously farsighted as she was concerned about cow's milk containing the TB virus which could be passed on to children. To protect her offspring, she took the precaution of giving them only goat's milk which does not carry the virus. As a result, goats were kept for that purpose as well as for their meat.

M
E
A
T

When my Grandfather killed a goat or kid for meat he would hang the meat as far down the well as possible, that being the coldest place. This was in the days before refrigeration had reached many island homes.

Nan du Feu told me that one of her sons, as a small boy, suffered from eczema on his hands. Nothing the doctor prescribed did any good, then she remembered that goat's milk was supposed to cure the condition. Sure enough, it cured John's eczema.

My parents kept goats for milk during the Occupation which we children had to drink. I'm sure they were scrupulously clean but to this day I can smell that strong scent of 'goat' with every glass we had to drink. My Mother sometimes used the milk to make junket, often colouring it pink with cochineal.

Goat's milk which hasn't been pasteurised is available. I have made curds using it and they are very good.

One is more likely to come across goat meat in Middle Eastern and Mediterranean countries. What is familiar is goat's cheese which is also still made locally.

This pure white cheese has a distinct flavour which can be quite strong. It is usually made in a small 'log' shape which is easy to use as it happily cuts into convenient rounds or it comes in small whole cheeses which are also adaptable.

Goat's Cheese Parcels

Serves 4
2 sheets of puff pastry - approx. 150g/8oz
4 slices goat's cheese (45g/1.5oz each parcel)
1 egg
16 basil leaves

The parcels are sufficient for one per person as a starter, double quantities for two each.

Cut each sheet of pastry in half. Roll out to about 15cms/6inches square. Place two basil leaves and a piece of cheese on each. Place two more basil leaves on top. With beaten egg, moisten the edges of the square. Draw up the opposite corners, squeezing the edges together. Brush with egg and bake in a hot oven 215°C, 425°F, Gas 7 for about fifteen minutes until golden.

Serve warm with a rocket salad or mixed green salad.

Goat's Cheese Salad

Serves 4

2 leeks
Carrots weighing about 150g/5oz
2 spring onions
1 tbsp chopped parsley
1 tbsp runny honey

1 tbsp lemon juice
2 tbsp olive oil
Salt and pepper
4 rounds of goat's cheese

Grate the carrot. Finely slice the leek, cover with boiling salted water, bring back to the boil for one minute. Drain and cool. When cool, place in a bowl with the carrot, finely sliced spring onion and parsley.

Make the vinaigrette by mixing the honey, lemon juice and olive oil. Mix with the leek and carrot mixture. Season. Pile a mound on four plates. Grill the cheese and, when bubbling, place a piece on top of each mound.

Roast Leg of Goat

This is roasted in the same way as a leg of lamb with slivers of garlic inserted into the flesh and a good scattering of herbs such as rosemary and thyme. It needs long, slow cooking in a moderate oven for three hours with regular basting.

M
E
A
T

Veal

Jersey French	*vieau* (m), *vée* (m)
Guernsey French	*viau* (m)

Unwanted calves, especially bull calves, are slaughtered for meat. Veal is still available and very good. It is pale in colour and has a delicate flavour. Very young veal is difficult to handle as the muscle fibres haven't firmed up, making the flesh soft. Stock and jelly made from a calf's foot is considered the best and is still used for both sweet and savoury dishes.

A favourite way of cooking veal is as an escalope – a thin slice of meat coated with egg and breadcrumbs and fried. This is served with a wedge of lemon and small pats of butter that have been mixed with chopped chives and parsley.

Calves' liver is a rarity but if you can get it, it is delicious. All it needs is a dusting of flour, before briefly frying in butter.

Veal & Ham Pie

Pies of all kinds are adaptable. They are ideal for picnics, supper parties, boating and so on as they are easily transported and their contents stay fresh within their firm pastry case. They are easily made. Don't be put off by pictures of elegant pies, tall and regal with fascinating decorations. They can be made in 2lb loaf tins or loose bottomed cake tins just as easily as in hinged, fluted tins. They are inexpensive to make but it is important to have a good pastry crust.

The following quantities are enough for a 1litre/2pint capacity tin or 22cm/9inch loose-bottomed cake tin:

1kilo/2lbs veal - alternatively use pork
250g/8oz unsmoked bacon pieces
250g/8oz belly of pork
1 tsp allspice
2 shallots or 1 medium onion finely chopped
1 tsp fresh thyme
1 tbsp brandy
Salt and pepper

Prepare the meat by cutting it into fairly small pieces. Put everything in a bowl and mix well. Leave for about an hour. In the meantime, make the pastry.

Hot-Water Crust Pastry
500g/1lb plain flour
250ml/8fl oz water
180g/6oz lard or Spry
Salt
1 egg for brushing the top of the pie
275ml/10fl oz aspic jelly

In the past, aspic jelly would have been made in the home but it can be difficult getting it the right consistency. Imagine the disappointment on cutting the beautiful pie and all the juices run out!

Place the flour in a roomy bowl, add a good pinch of salt making a well in the centre.

Bring the water and lard to the boil, pour into the well and using a wooden spoon mix, then knead until you have a smooth ball using a little extra flour if necessary.

While still warm and pliable, keep a quarter for the lid. Form the pastry into a ball, flatten it with your hands or use a rolling pin until the pastry is big enough to come up the sides of the tin. Press it firmly into the tin.

Fill the pie with the ready prepared meat. Moisten the edge of the pastry then place the lid on top, crimping the edges to seal it.

Make a hole in the middle and place a rolled up piece of card into it. This will allow steam to escape and will be a useful funnel to pour in the jellied aspic. Brush the top with beaten egg.

Bake for thirty minutes at 200°C, 400°F, Gas 6 then reduce the heat to 165°C, 325°F, Gas 3 for two hours, checking after the first hour in case the top needs to be covered with foil.

Make the aspic according to the instructions, then cool it. As soon as the pie comes out of the oven, pour a little of the aspic jelly into the pie so that it sinks to the bottom. Gradually add the rest of the aspic as the pie cools. When the pie has cooled remove from the tin.

M
E
A
T

Veal with Mushrooms

Serves 4
1 kilo/2lbs veal
120g/4oz smoked bacon
12 shallots or small onions
16 button mushrooms
2 egg yolks
90ml/3fl oz double cream
3 bay leaves
4/5 cloves or half tsp ground cloves
30g/1oz butter
1 tbsp chopped parsley
Salt and pepper

Fry the shallots in the butter, followed by the mushrooms and bacon, put to one side.

Cut the veal into pieces and fry in the butter until all the liquid has evaporated and the meat is golden brown. Place in an ovenproof casserole with the shallots, mushrooms, bacon, bay leaves and cloves. Season. Cover with water and cook in a moderate oven for an hour and a half. Mix the egg yolks and cream. Stir into the casserole, sprinkle with chopped parsley and serve.

Duck

Jersey French	*cannard* (m)
Guernsey French	*piràtte* (f) hp, *piraette* (f) lp

I have included duck although local duck is unlikely to be available now. Duckling becomes duck at about six weeks old. The meat is darker and stronger in flavour than chicken.

Duck goes very well with orange, turnips, red cabbage and sour cream.

Roast Duck with Sage & Onion Stuffing

Serves 4
A duck weighing 2-2.5 kilos/4-5 lbs

Sage & Onion Stuffing

4/5 sage leaves	Salt and pepper
1 onion	120g/4oz fresh breadcrumbs
30g/1oz butter and a little	1 lemon
extra for the breast before cooking	1 tbsp flour

Blanch the sage leaves in boiling water. Put the breadcrumbs, finely chopped onion and sage leaves in a bowl. Add the grated lemon rind, melted butter, salt and pepper. Mix until it sticks together using a little of the lemon juice if necessary. Fill the duck's cavity.

If there are giblets, simmer them to make stock for the gravy.

Place the duck in a roasting pan, season with salt and pepper. Spread the butter on the breast. Roast at 190°C, 375°F, Gas 5 for an hour and a half, basting every thirty minutes.

Remove the bird from the pan and keep warm. Drain off most of the fat. Scrape the bits off the pan, add one tbsp flour, mix together and make the gravy either with the giblet stock or water.

M
E
A
T

Duck with Orange

Serves 4

4 duck breasts	1 tbsp wine vinegar
2 oranges	8 shallots
1 lemon	30g/1oz flour
4tbsp thick marmalade	60g/2oz butter
275ml/5fl oz Madeira or white wine	Salt and pepper

Trim the breasts of any excess fat. Mix the wine vinegar, marmalade, juice from an orange and a lemon in a large bowl. Take the four duck breasts. Score them at an angle and coat with the mixture. Leave to marinate for thirty minutes, turning occasionally.

While the breasts marinate, slice the second orange into eight thin slices. Fry these gently in half the butter until soft and bronzed. Remove from the pan and keep warm.

Keeping the marinade to one side, fry the duck breasts in the same pan using the remaining butter until golden and well cooked, about fifteen minutes on each side. Place in a serving dish and keep warm.

Tip most of the fat out of the pan, then fry the sliced shallots. Sprinkle with flour, adding the marinade and Madeira. Season and stirring, bring to the boil.

To serve, place two slices of orange on each breast and pour the sauce over and around.

Jersey Royal Potatoes

Jersey French	*des rouoyals*	
Guernsey French	*des patates tempreunnes* (f pl) earlies	

Jersey Royals deserve a chapter to themselves as they are unique. For this reason the States of Jersey have protected them. They have a Designation of Origin status and proof must be available showing where they were grown. Since their development, they have been grown in earth enriched with seaweed, farm manure and, later on, guano. Jersey's mild climate and longer days meant they had an early start on potatoes grown in England. Almost every scrap of land was used to plant them, from the back doorstep to the steep slopes or cotîls where only goats would normally be happy.

The potato was first planted in quantities around 1800. It is on record that 600 tons left Jersey in 1807 but, by the early 1900s, over 2,000 tons were exported annually, increasing to 30,000 in 1939. With the success of the potato, apple orchards were uprooted and fields where parsnips were grown were turned over to it. Another reason for the demise of the apple and parsnip was that, after the potatoes had been lifted, tomatoes could be planted. But it wasn't all plain sailing as the potato blight of 1845 and many years after caused ruin for many.

Fortunately, men like farmer John Le Caudey and Hugh de la Haye experimented with different potatoes. Eventually Charles Le Feuvre discovered an early variety which he named the Royal Jersey Fluke. The dictionary describes a 'fluke' as an accidental success which sums up the name perfectly! It is small, has a unique flavour, with a paper-thin skin and creamy flesh. It seems it can't be grown elsewhere, even a Jersey Royal grown in Guernsey doesn't have the same flavour as its Jersey brother!

Sadly, over the years the flavour has very often suffered. There could be many reasons – perhaps the use of artificial fertilisers or the forcing under polythene or glass. These methods are used in a bid to get the Jersey Royal on the market earlier and earlier. Fortunately, there are growers who are keen to preserve its quality and who insist on growing them slowly and as naturally as possible in the time-honoured way. These potatoes are superior.

Many of the small growers who once depended on the Royal for a living have been forced out of business, their small parcels of land unable to support a family. The weather can also be unpredictable; for example during the Spring of 2003 a severe frost almost sounded the death knell of the crop.

V
E
G
E
T
A
B
L
E
S

There is only one way to cook Jersey Royals.

They should be boiled with sprigs of mint in salted water. On serving, a spoonful of butter added to the pan and the potatoes rolled around. They go with any and everything.

~

Jersey Cabbage

Jersey French   *Chour Jersiais* (m)

Like the Jersey Royal, the bizarre Jersey Cabbage is unique to the island. Nicknamed 'Long Jack', the Jersey Cabbage has been cultivated since the early 1800s and can attain a height of 20 feet (almost 6 metres). It has a rather scabious stalk about 5cms/2 inches in diameter. The stalk has many uses. It can be dried, hardened and polished to make a very attractive walking stick or used to support outdoor tomato plants. The leaves are primarily used as cattle fodder but may be used in the kitchen as well. It seems the more the leaves are picked the taller grows the cabbage!

During our visit to Hamptonne, a restored cluster of farm buildings, we learned that bread dough was wrapped in cabbage leaves before being baked. In the past, the bottom of the bread had been burnt black by the hot bricks forming the base of the oven. This, we were told, was cut off and given to the workers while the 'upper crust' went to the house! It was good to learn that, even now, there is a demand for bread baked in this way which bakeries are meeting.

Bread baked in a Cabbage Leaf

1 small cabbage
500g/1lb strong bread flour
2 tsp salt
2 level tsp dried yeast
Half tsp sugar
About 275ml/10fl oz warm water
Knob of butter

Put a little of the water in a bowl. Sprinkle over the dried yeast and sugar. Leave for five minutes to bubble.

In a roomy bowl, put the flour and salt. Rub in the butter then add the yeast and water until you have a fairly sticky dough. Knead until smooth and soft. Place the bowl in a plastic bag and allow to prove in a warm place for two hours.

Tip onto a floured board, knock it down and knead again, shaping into a ball.

Take three or four cabbage leaves. Cut out the ribs so that the leaves are flat. Arrange them on a round sandwich baking tin. Put the dough on top and draw the leaves up and over. Bake in a hot oven 220°C, 425°F, Gas 7 for thirty to forty minutes.

~

Seakale

Jersey French   *chou mathîn*

I first became aware of seakale when reading *Les Travailleurs de la Mer/The Toilers of the Sea.* Victor Hugo extolled its virtues and he described Gilliatt digging a trench for seakale in his garden at Bu de la Rue.

Seakale grows wild on the seashore in places such as Les Pezeries in Guernsey. There we have collected wild seed pods. We have also used 'thongs' so that now we have a healthy patch both from the thongs as well as from the wild seed pods.

The transition of the wild plant took place in the early eighteenth century and was very popular as a vegetable with the Victorians. Then it went out of fashion and has only recently been revived. It is a strange vegetable needing care

V
E
G
E
T
A
B
L
E
S

and attention. Once the young shoots start to appear, forcing pots are placed over them to keep the stalks white. They are ready to pick when they are about 20 cms/8 inches long They look rather like a smoother version of celery with green curly bits at the top.

Seakale is cooked in the same way as asparagus. It has a delicate flavour which is best enjoyed by serving accompanied with a simple vinaigrette or Hollandaise sauce.

Seakale with Hollandaise Sauce

Serves 4

120g/4oz seakale per person

Sauce

3 tbsp white wine vinegar

4 black peppercorns

3 tbsp water

1 bayleaf

180g/6oz unsalted butter

Salt

Cook the seakale in boiling salted water for five minutes.

Make the sauce by boiling the wine, water, peppercorns and bay leaf until reduced to one tbsp.

If making by hand, place a bowl in a saucepan of barely simmering water. Add the egg yolks and cooled reduced liquid. Thoroughly mix then little by little add the butter. Season with salt.

If you aren't going to use it straight away, cover and remove from the heat, stirring now and again to keep it smooth and creamy.

To make it in a food processor: put in the egg yolks, start whizzing, adding the reduced liquid. In a steady stream, add the melted butter. Place the creamy mixture in a bowl, season with salt and cover with cling film or foil and place in a pan of warm (not hot) water. Stir occasionally to keep it smooth and creamy.

Share the seakale between four plates, pouring the hollandaise sauce over.

Seakale with Vinaigrette

Seakale, I feel, should be served on its own to appreciate its special flavour.

Serves 4
120g/4oz seakale per person
1 tbsp lemon juice
275ml/5fl oz olive oil + 1 tbsp
1 tsp french mustard
Salt and pepper
30g/1oz toasted chopped walnuts

Cook the seakale in boiling salted water for five minutes. Drain and cool.

In a small bowl mix the mustard and lemon juice. Gradually add the olive oil until well mixed. Season and add the finely chopped walnuts. Pour over the seakale.

~

Calabrese

Calabrese is grown very successfully throughout the islands. It is harvested throughout the year except during the summer months. Really fresh calabrese is a beautiful dark green with a bluish tinge. This versatile vegetable is a favourite as it goes with almost everything. Care must be taken not to overcook it otherwise its delicate flavour is lost. Boiling in salted water for four minutes is sufficient.

V
E
G
E
T
A
B
L
E
S

Spring Cabbage

Jersey French	*caboche* (f), *d'ernouvé* (m)
Guernsey French	*caboche* (f), *d'nouvé* (m)

Spring cabbage can be mistaken for a young cabbage but it is a variety all of its own. It begins to appear towards the end of April but its season is short. It is easily recognised as it is quite pointed.

Shredded and plunged into boiling salted water for a couple of minutes is all that is needed. Strained and tossed in butter it is very tasty.

Bubble & Squeak

Bubble and Squeak is traditionally made with leftover vegetables but is far superior if made freshly with cabbage and potatoes. It goes with almost everything and is extra special with eggs cracked on top five minutes before serving – HP sauce too!

Serves 4
750g/1.5lbs potatoes
A small or half a cabbage
  (about 500g/1lb of prepared cabbage)
60g/2oz butter
2-3 tbsp full cream milk
Salt and pepper

Boil the potatoes and cabbage separately in salted water until cooked. Drain both.

Mash the potato, adding the butter and milk. Chop the cabbage and add to the potato. Mix thoroughly. To get the bubble to squeak, it should be cooked in a frying pan. Put a knob of butter or dripping into the pan and when really hot, spoon in the cabbage and potato, pressing it down. Soon it will begin to bubble and squeak. After five minutes, cut into quarters turning each quarter and pressing them to form one piece. At this stage, you can crack and cook some eggs on top.

Elder

Jersey French	*seu* (m)
Guernsey French	*d'la saeue* (f)

Marie De Garis describes the Elder as a sacred tree. During a thunderstorm it was considered a safe refuge as it wouldn't be struck by lightning. It was also a protection against witchcraft and was planted near the dairy window to prevent witches flying in and interfering with the butter making.

It contains many medicinal virtues. The inner bark relieves burns. A decoction of the flowers, *d'la flleur de saeue*, improves the complexion and removes freckles. Old people made an infusion to ease stomach pains; wine made from the berries soothes a sore throat. Not only has the elder many virtues but it looks and smells lovely as the clusters of white flowers open. Then later in the summer, clusters of black juicy berries hang from its branches.

Apart from its medicinal uses, the highly scented sprays of flowers, which start appearing during May, make delicious cordials and puddings. Elder flowers go well with gooseberries.

The berries are good in pies, jams and chutneys and can be picked and dried for use in recipes. They must have been very welcome during the Occupation with food shortages.

Elderberries should always be cooked because they are mildly toxic in a raw state.

WILD FOOD

Elder Flower Cordial/ Champagne

This recipe was given to me by a well known ond loved Guernsey lady, Viv Mansell.

The reason for the champagne title is that it is slightly effervescent. Place four or five freshly picked heads into a bowl or basin. Make sure the flowers have unfurled as they will be at their best. Pour over 2 litres/4 pints of cold water, adding 375g/12oz granulated sugar, 1 tbsp white wine vinegar and the rind and juice of a lemon. Stir occasionally to dissolve the sugar.

After 24 hours, strain and bottle, preferably in glass bottles with screw tops. It will be ready to drink in two weeks but better if left a little longer – up to six months. Care must be taken over its storage. A word of advice – store it in a cupboard as it can go off with a bang!

Elder Flower Syrup

Perhaps a safer bet than the champagne as it won't explode.

Pick about eighteen heads of open unfurled flowers.

Put 550ml/1pt water in a pan. Add 250g/ 8oz granulated sugar. As it comes slowly to the boil, snip the heads in, pushing them down. Once boiling point is reached and the sugar is dissolved, cover and put to one side until cold. Strain the juice returning it to the pan. Boil to reduce it by half. Add the strained juice of a lemon then bottle.

Refrigerated, it should keep for at least a month and can be used in puddings, cakes, custards and sauces.

Elder Flower Creams

Serves 4
275ml/10fl oz double cream
2 eggs + 2 egg yolks
2 tbsp elder flower syrup

Beat together the eggs, yolks and cream. Add the syrup. Pour into four well buttered ramekins and cover with foil. Place in a roasting tin with water coming half way up. Cook in a moderate oven 180°C, 350°F, Gas 4 for about thirty minutes. If they are still a bit wobbly it doesn't matter as they will firm up on getting cold and will be deliciously creamy. Refrigerate then turn out and surround with rhubarb purée.

W
I
L
D

F
O
O
D

Elder Flower Fritters

Serves 4
4 stems elder flowers (more depending on size)
 - keep the stem to use as a handle
90 gm/3oz flour
1 egg
150ml/5fl oz water
Oil for frying
Castor sugar
Mint

Make the batter by whisking the egg with the flour and half water. When smooth, add the rest of the water.

Check the stems and flower for dust and if necessary gently shake. Don't wash as this removes a lot of the fragrance. Dip the flowers in the batter, gently shaking off any excess. Fry in oil until golden brown, taking great care in case they splutter. Drain on kitchen paper. Scatter each plate with sugar and torn mint leaves and place the fritter on top with a wedge of lemon alongside.

F
R
U
I
T

Rhubarb

| Jersey French | *rhubarbe* (f) |
| Guernsey French | *rhubarbe* (f) |

The red/green stalks are probably the first fruit to appear in Spring. Often it was forced by placing barrels or forcing pots over the clumps but I think the flavour is better if the rhubarb is left to grow naturally. Until the nineteenth century, rhubarb was used mainly as a laxative but it slowly became popular as a food. Rhubarb was not always liked by children when it was stewed to a pulp and accompanied by custard or rice pudding. Hopefully, most of us grow out of this childish dislike! Rhubarb is delicious and its astringent flavour gives a liveliness to crumbles and mousses. It also marries well with ginger and makes an excellent sauce to accompany, say, mackerel.

Rhubarb Tart

Serves 6-9 depending on size of portions
A rectangular baking tin 30 x 23 cms or 12 x 9 inches
375g/12oz flour
250g/8oz butter   1 kilo/2lbs rhubarb
180g/6oz sugar   1 tsp ground ginger

Make the shortcrust pastry by rubbing or grating the butter into the flour until it resembles fine breadcrumbs. Add water and mix to a stiff dough. Using just over half of the dough, roll and line the baking tin. Cut the washed and trimmed rhubarb into short pieces and spread over the pastry. Sprinkle over the sugar and ground ginger. Roll out the second half of pastry and cover the rhubarb, sealing the edges. Brush with milk or water and sprinkle with a little sugar. Mark into portions with a knife. Bake in a moderate oven, 190°C, 375°F, Gas 5 for thirty to forty minutes.

Rhubarb & Orange Crumble

Serves 6

1 kilo/2lb rhubarb
1 tbsp runny honey
2 oranges

120g/4oz Demerara sugar
120g/4oz butter
120g/4oz flour

Grate the oranges finely and squeeze the juice. Mix the juice and honey.

Cut the rhubarb into 2cm/1inch pieces and place in an oven-proof dish. Pour over the juice and honey. Add half the sugar. Grate the butter into the flour. Add the remaining sugar and grated peel. Cover the rhubarb with the mixture. Cook in a moderate oven, 190°C, 375°F, Gas 5 for thirty-five to forty minutes.

Serve with good old fashioned Bird's Custard.

Rhubarb & Ginger Fool

Serves 4

500g/1lb rhubarb
2 tsp gelatine
150ml/5fl oz double cream
120g/4oz granulated sugar

2-3 pieces of preserved ginger
 in syrup
Cochineal (optional)

Trim and wash the rhubarb, cut into small pieces and stew with the sugar in a little water, about two tbsp. In a small bowl or teacup, sprinkle the gelatine onto three tbsp. of tepid water. Leave to dissolve. It may be necessary to stand the bowl in hot water to help the gelatine dissolve.

Once the rhubarb is cooked, sieve into a bowl. Chop the ginger into very small pieces and add to the rhubarb. Fold in the gelatine and cochineal for a pinker colour. Allow to cool. Whip the cream until soft and gently fold into the rhubarb mixture. Spoon into four glasses. Refrigerate until set.

M
I
L
K

Milk – our Golden Liquor

| Jersey French | *lait* (m) |
| Guernsey French | *lait* (m) |

We are lucky to have such wonderful milk which tastes better than any other I have tried. Our milk is renowned throughout the world for its flavour, richness, creaminess and golden colour. The colour is due to the carotene in the grass which is absorbed into the cow's system. It can't digest and eliminate it as other breeds do.

In Springtime the milk is especially rich as the cattle feed on new, lush young grass and calves are born, stimulating the production of large quantities of delicious milk. Nowadays, great care is taken over hygiene on the farm and in the dairy. Even with pasteurisation, our milk is still the best.

The collection, pasteurisation and distribution of milk is undertaken by the States Dairies in Jersey and Guernsey. In Alderney and Sark, individual pasteurisation machines are used. Pasteurisation ensures the milk is free of certain germs and less apt to sour. Fortunately, pasteurisation doesn't affect the making of cheese, butter and cream. Butter and cream are as rich in colour and texture as they have always been.

In my childhood days, I remember my mother making curds or cream cheese from unpasteurised milk that had gone off.

It was also used for baking and a favourite dish was new potatoes with sour milk. The sour milk was poured over the hot potatoes and the dish was eaten like a kind of soup.

Butter - the Golden Fat of the Land

| Jersey French | du beurre (m) |
| Guernsey French | du burre (m) |

Butter has been made from antiquity. Local farms took great pride in their butter and purity was very important. It was also important to ensure that milk for butter making came from cows grazing the best pasture – butter from cows fed on turnips or poor pasture was inevitably inferior, even rancid.

Like butter, cream was always another important by-product of milk but, today, we have such a wide variety that the following explanation may be helpful:

Double Cream has 48% fat. When very fresh it tends to be runny but thickens as it ages. It can be treated with heat and sold as thick or extra thick cream.

Single Cream has 18-20% fat which is too low for whipping.

Extra Thick Cream has 38% fat.

Whipping Cream has 38% fat with a foamy quality on whipping.

Crème Fraîche has 40% fat. This slightly fermented cream is very popular as it can be boiled without curdling. It is thick enough to be spooned without any whipping and its taste is less cloying than double cream.

Sour Cream has 18% fat but seems to have given way to crème fraîche.

Clotted Cream has 60% fat. The cream has been heated or scalded so that it becomes thick, keeps longer but has a slightly 'cooked' taste.

Reduced Fat Cream has the addition of stabilisers and thickeners.

Fromage Frais, sometimes known as Fromage Blanc, is usually included with this range of dairy products. It is a light white cheese that has been slightly fermented with a varying fat content, usually very low. It is smooth with an almost pouring consistency. It can be used for sweet and savoury dishes and is lighter as it contains less cream.

I suggest sticking to straightforward single or double cream or crème fraîche if a hint of sourness is desired.

Light Cream Cheese

275ml/half pint double cream
275ml/half pint full cream milk
2tsp rennet

In a pan, just warm the milk and cream until tepid. Stir in the rennet and leave for three hours. Ladle the soft, slippery curd into a muslin cloth (lay the cloth across a colander over a bowl), add a little salt. Leave to drain up to six hours.

This quantity will make about 180g/250g; 6oz/8oz cream cheese.

Curds

Jersey French   *du lait cailli êputtié* (m)
Guernsey French   *des Caillebottes* (f pl)

Milk set aside for butter making also produced the best curds, being creamier and golden in colour. Curds were produced as well from the buttermilk left over after the butter making process was finished. Nothing was wasted as the remaining colourless whey was used for feeding young calves and piglets.

To make curds, unpasteurised milk is needed. Sadly, gone are the days of bowls full of the crumbly curd scattered with sugar, a grating of nutmeg and cream or milk.

Orange Cream Cheese Tart

Serves 8

Pastry
180g/6oz plain flour
120g/4oz butter
2 tbsp water

Filling
60g/2oz sugar
2 eggs
1 orange
30g/1oz candied orange peel
Grated nutmeg
350g/12oz cream cheese - fromage frais is lighter than Philadelphia

Make the pastry in the usual way and line a 20cm/8inch flan tin. Bake blind at 190°C, 375°F, Gas 5 for fifteen minutes.

Put the cream cheese in a bowl. Add the sugar, beaten eggs, grated orange peel, juice of half the orange and finely chopped candied orange peel. Mix well and pour into the pastry case. Grate or sprinkle the nutmeg over the surface.

Bake at 190°C, 375°F, Gas 5 for about thirty minutes until just set. Even if it still a bit wobbly it doesn't matter as, on cooling, it firms up but is still creamy.

M
I
L
K

Custard Tart

Custard tarts with their creamy concave filling are rarely seen nowadays which is a pity.
Quantities are for ten muffin sized tarts or 20cm/8inch ovenproof flan dish.

Pastry
180g/6oz plain flour
120g/4oz butter
2 tbsp water

Filling
275ml/10fl oz full cream milk
30g/1oz caster sugar
1 egg + 2 yolks
1 bay leaf
Grated nutmeg

Make the pastry and line a 20cm/8inch flan or pie dish or muffin tin for individual ones – a thickish pastry is needed.

Heat the milk with the bay leaf and sugar until the sugar has dissolved.

In a bowl, beat the egg and yolks, stir in the milk, removing the bay leaf. Pour into the pastry case. Scatter with the grated nutmeg. Bake at 190°C, 375°F, Gas 5 for thirty minutes until set and pastry is cooked.

M
I
L
K

Crème Brulée

Serves 4

4 egg yolks
500ml/10fl oz double cream
90ml/3fl oz full cream milk

Vanilla pod
90g/3oz caster sugar + 6 tbsp
  for the crust

Whisk the egg yolks, cream and sugar until pale and creamy. Add the milk. Split the vanilla pod, scrape out and add the seeds to the creamy mixture. Spoon into four ramekins and place them in a roasting tin. Pour boiling water so that it comes half way up the ramekins. Cook at 190°C, 375°F, Gas 5 for about forty-five minutes until set. Remove from the water. Cover with foil and when cool, refrigerate until needed.

Just before serving, cover the surface with sugar. Place under a hot grill until the sugar caramelises, about five or six minutes, or use a blow torch.

Cream Cup & Saucers

Makes 6

425ml/15fl oz double cream
150ml/5fl oz full cream milk
100g/3oz castor sugar

Lemon peel from half a lemon
2 tbsp Calvados
4 tsp powdered gelatine or
  1 x 12g packet

In a small bowl scatter the gelatine onto three tbsp tepid water. To help it dissolve, stand the bowl in a pan of hot water.

Bring the cream and peel from the lemon to almost boiling point. Stir in the sugar and leave to infuse for thirty minutes. Heat the milk but don't boil. Add the dissolved gelatine then leave to cool. Remove the lemon peel and slowly stir the cream into the milk and gelatine followed by the Calvados. Pour into six very lightly oiled ramekins, moulds or teacups. Refrigerate until needed. Gently invert the moulds onto plates surrounding the creamy mounds with a purée of fresh fruit.

Wedding Breakfast Baking

Jersey French   *dêjeuner* (m); *dé neuches* (f pl)
Guernsey French: *les r'neuchaons*

As it is Spring, I will describe a Wedding Breakfast. Weddings can take place at any time of the year but they seem to be very popular around Easter.

The solemnity of the service will be followed by much gaiety and happiness but it is also a time for feasting! The daily routine of hard work is forgotten.

Weddings have and always will be happy events with excited preparation beforehand. They can also be a time for healing family rifts!

In the past and now, tremendous trouble is taken over preparations.

In the country, if the house was too small for all the invited guests, a barn would be emptied and prepared.

Eventually the great day arrives. The service over, the bride along with her trousseau (which she had been working on for months) is on the eve of leaving her home but she leaves with the warmth and goodwill of her family.

In the past it was very often the custom for someone in the family to plant a myrtle tree at the gate of the bride's new home. Greek legend tells us that myrtle is the tree of love, fertility and good luck so a good omen for the newly-weds.

Weddings followed a traditional pattern with little changing until the 1900s, especially in the country parishes.

The furze oven/*le grànd four* worked overtime as *viands* – meats consisting of ham, pork and beef and *des houichepottes*/puddings were cooked.

On tables, meats alongside vegetables and chutneys jostled for space with puddings and various gâches made with sultanas, currants, raisins or just butter. Cakes too nestled alongside plates piled high with buttered *galëttes* – biscuits. All was washed down with cider, beer, mulled wine, lemonade and tea.

Feasting over, it would be time for perhaps a fiddle and accordion to be brought out. During the junketing, plates of *gâche*, apple cake and *galëttes* topped with butter and cheese would be offered from wicker baskets which were normally used to take butter to market. Once again all was washed down with a choice of beverages.

Gâche

The women of the house took great pride in their baking. There are very many recipes so this is a good opportunity to include some of them.

Gâche is the Norman French word for cake. It is an enriched bread as yeast is always used. Sultanas, raisins, currants and mixed peel are usually included or it can be plain. Our butter gives it its unique flavour.

Many recipes include brown and white sugar, wholemeal flour and eggs. Quantities of fruit vary too. Recipes vary from place to place, having evolved over time, so what is traditional in one parish may not be so in another.

Basic Recipe

500g/1lb plain flour (many recipes use 750g/1lb 8oz flour)
250g/8oz butter
310g/10oz dried currants, sultanas or raisins plus 60g/2oz mixed
  peel. Alternatively, leave out the mixed peel but increase the fruit.
15g/half oz fresh yeast or 2 tsp dried yeast or 1 pkt dried yeast
1 tsp sugar
Pinch of salt
150ml/5fl oz milk or water

If using fresh yeast, place in a bowl with one tsp sugar, add a little tepid milk and stir until dissolved. Add the rest of the milk and leave to become frothy. If using dried yeast, place the tepid milk in a bowl with one tsp sugar, sprinkle on the yeast and leave to become frothy. Use packeted yeast according to instructions.

Grate or rub the butter into the flour and salt. When the yeast is frothy, add to the mixture and mix to a soft dough; if on the dry side, add a little more milk or water. Knead for at least five minutes so that the dough becomes soft and smooth. Add the fruit, kneading again until it is well mixed in. I find it is easier to knead the dough before adding the fruit.

Place the bowl in a plastic bag as this helps the dough to rise or just cover with a tea towel. Leave in a warm place to rise for about two hours until the dough is double in size. Turn onto a floured board, knead once more. Place in a buttered tin, approximately 23cm/9inches by 18cms/7inches. Leave for twenty minutes to rise a second time. Bake for forty-five minutes to one hour in a moderate oven 200°C, 400°F, Gas 6.

Apple Pudding better known as Gâche Mêlaïe

Recipes are many and varied. This one was taken from *Guernsey Dishes of Bygone Days*, collected by J.Stevens-Cox.

It is Mrs Louisa Helmot's written in the eighteenth century. Her recipe said 1lb of sugar but I have reduced it.

Serves 8

500gl1lb plain flour
500g/1lb cooking apples
180g/6oz sugar
3 eggs

250g/8oz butter or suet
Half tsp ground nutmeg
1 tsp ground cinnamon

Peel and chop the apples. Scatter them in an ovenproof dish.

Sieve the flour and spices into a bowl. Rub or grate in the butter or suet. Add the sugar and beaten eggs. Stir until well mixed. If the mixture is too stiff, add a little milk. Spread over the apples and bake at 180°C, 350°F, Gas 4, for about an hour. Serve with cream or custard.

My second recipe is from La Société Guernesiaise – the higher proportion of apples in this recipe produces a moister result than Mrs Helmot's, given above.

Serves 6

1 kilo/2lbs cooking apples
250g/8oz flour
120g/4oz suet, lard or butter
120g/4oz sugar

Put the flour in a roomy bowl and grate in the suet, lard or butter. Add the sugar then the peeled and finely chopped apples. Mix well, then tip into a buttered ovenproof dish or tin. Bake at 190'C, 375°F, Gas 5 for thirty to forty minutes.

Apple Cake

500g/1lb Bramley or other cooking apples – about two good sized ones
250g/8oz self-raising flour

1 level tsp cinnamon

Half level tsp mixed spice

Half level tsp ground ginger

180g/6oz sultanas

60g/2oz mixed peel

60g/2oz raisins

60g/2oz chopped walnuts

90g/3oz glace ginger

180g/6oz butter

180g/6oz brown sugar

1 lemon

3 eggs

Grease and line a 20cm/8 inch cake tin.

Peel and cook the chopped apple in very little water until it collapses and is a thick purée.

Cream the finely grated lemon peel, sugar and butter. Add the beaten eggs one at a time. Add the fruit, chopped walnuts and ginger. Add the seived flour and spices alternately with the apple. Bake at 165°C, 325°F, Gas 3 for an hour and a quarter. Test to see if it is cooked. Cool in the tin.

Cider Cakes: Gâche à Cidre

These can be made as cup cakes or as one whole cake in an 18cm/7inch round tin.

250g/8oz soft brown sugar

180g/6oz butter

180g/6oz sultanas

1 lemon

250g/8oz self-raising flour

1 tsp ground cinnamon

2 eggs

150ml/5fl oz dry cider

Soak the sultanas in the cider for about thirty minutes or until they have plumped up.

Cream the sugar and butter. Add the finely grated lemon peel and beaten eggs. Mix well, then add the sieved flour and spice and finally the sultanas and cider.

Either bake in paper cases or as a cake at 180°C, 350°F, Gas 4, about twenty minutes for the individual cakes or forty-five minutes to one hour for a cake.

Seed Cake: d'la Zîtchêke

As a child I never enjoyed my mother's seed cakes but am happy that I have now acquired the taste!

This is another eighteenth century recipe which I have adapted from *Guernsey Dishes of Bygone Days*.

RECETTE PR. DES CIDE CAKES

1lb Beure	1lb butter
1lb Farrine	1lb flour
1lb de Sucre	1lb sugar
12 Oeufs en autant la moitie des Blanc	12 eggs plus half as many whites
Un Verre d'Eau Rose	A glass of rose water
Un Verre d'Eau de Vie	A glass of brandy
Du Carraway	Some caraway

One thing that surprised me was that the quantities are in English weights, as it is an eighteenth century recipe and French was then the spoken language.

I have adapted the above recipe to make a cake baked in a loaf tin, 22cm/8.5inch by 11cm/4.5inch

180g/6oz butter
250g/8oz self-raising flour
180g/6oz castor sugar
3 eggs

1 tbsp rose water
1 tbsp brandy
1 level tbsp caraway seed

Cream the butter and sugar. Add the beaten eggs one at a time. Fold in the sieved flour, caraway seed, brandy and rose water until a soft consistency. Spoon into the buttered tin. Bake at 165°C, 325°F, Gas 3 for one hour. Cool, then turn onto a wire rack.

This same recipe can be adapted for a Madeira cake but without the caraway. Instead add the finely grated peel of one lemon to the creamed butter and sugar and, after forty-five minutes cooking, place two pieces of candied lemon peel on top of the cake.

Jersey Wonders: des Mèrvelles

I remember going to Miriam Paint's house in St Peter's in Guernsey to see Jersey Wonders being made. The way they were twisted looked a bit complicated, but the end result was really good. Brown on the outside but, on being broken open, a yellow buttery texture was revealed which tasted delicious. They weren't in the slightest bit greasy from the frying either.

There are several recipes in the *Buoun Appétit* booklet produced by the Jersey Women's Institute. During my visit to Jersey I met Mrs Eileen Le Sueur. What a wonderful person – so full of interesting things to tell us about her life and her love of her native island.

This is her recipe. One thing she insisted upon was kneading the dough until smooth, even if it takes ten minutes, otherwise it can crumble on cooking.

This quantity makes obout 12 wonders

500g/1lb self-raising flour
120g/4oz butter or margarine
180g/6oz sugar
4 eggs
Lard or oil for frying

Sieve the flour into a bowl. Grate or rub in the butter. Add the beaten eggs and sugar. Mix to a soft paste. Knead until smooth. Divide into twelve pieces and roll into balls. Taking one at a time, gently roll into an oblong shape. Cut a slit down the length. Take the ends, encouraging them through the slit so that you have a twisted shape. Fry in hot oil or lard, about one minute on each side.

The wonders can be twisted into different shapes such as butterflies or figures of eight. I got into a real tangle so stuck to a figure of eight and they were delicious.

I loved the comment in the Jersey Women's Institute book *Buoun Appétit*. According to certain people, the state of the tide has much to do with the success of their Wonders. It is to our knowledge that more than one housewife takes good care to make her Wonders when the sea is going down.

Jersey/Guernsey Biscuits: des Galëttes

750g/1lb 8oz strong plain flour	1 tsp sugar
250g/8oz butter	425ml/15fl oz warm water
2 tsp dried yeast or half oz fresh yeast	Pinch of salt

In a small bowl, pour half the warm water, stir in the sugar and sprinkle the yeast on top. Alternatively cream the fresh yeast with the sugar, add a little water then leave for five minutes to begin working.

Put the flour and salt in a roomy bowl (I use a plastic washing up bowl). Grate in the butter. When the yeast is bubbling, add to the flour and knead adding more water until the dough is smooth, about ten minutes. The dough must be soft and pliable, a dough that is too stiff will never rise. Place in a plastic bag and leave to rise for about an hour and a half to two hours.

Divide into twelve pieces. Knead each one into a round, make a hole in the centre by inserting your finger to produce the typical 'dimple' in the finished product. Place on a greased tray. Bake in a hot oven, 220°C, 425°F, Gas 7 for fifteen to twenty minutes.

Gâche à Fouée

These thickish flat discs of bread dough were cooked in front of the fire while the bread was cooking in the oven. They were spread with butter and eaten hot. Like the galëttes, a finger was inserted in the middle before baking for the 'dimple' effect.

WEDDING BREAKFAST BAKING

Des Fliottes

This filling Jersey speciality was traditionally cooked and eaten on Good Friday in many homes. This recipe is from the Jersey WI booklet, *Buoun Appétit*.

250g/8oz flour
1litre/2 pints milk
120g/4oz sugar

2 eggs
knob of butter
pinch of salt

Mix the flour, salt and sugar. Add the beaten eggs and sufficient milk to make a thick batter. Bring the milk to the boil then add the knob of butter. Carefully spoon in one tbsp. of batter, allowing room for them to float. Cook for several minutes.

Serve hot sprinkled with sugar and with some of the milk.

Hot Cross Buns

Whilst it is generally held that Hot Cross Buns are a reminder of the Crucifixion, others maintain that the cross is cut into the rising dough to let the devil fly out!

To make 12 buns
500g/1lb strong white flour
1 level tsp salt
2 level tsp dried yeast
Half level tsp mixed spice
Half level tsp ground cinnamon
Half level tsp ground nutmeg
120g/4oz currants

60g/2oz chopped mixed peel
60g/2oz castor sugar
60g/2oz butter
150ml/5fl oz warm milk and water
1 egg
Glaze
2 tbsp milk, water and castor sugar

Pour a little of the water and milk mixture into a small bowl. Sprinkle the dried yeast on top and add a little sugar. Leave for about five minutes to bubble.

In a roomy basin sieve the flour and spices making a well in the centre. Beat the egg and add, along with the fruit, peel, melted butter and sugar. Mix to a sticky dough with the remaining milk and water. Knead the dough with a little flour if necessary until it is smooth. Place the bowl in a plastic bag and leave to prove for an hour and a half until double in size.

Turn the dough onto a floured board, knock it down and divide into twelve portions. Shape into buns, cutting a cross on each. Place on a greased baking tray. Leave to rise until puffy, about twenty minutes. Bake at 220°C, 425°F, Gas 7 for fifteen to twenty minutes.

While they are cooking, make the glaze. Boil the milk, water and sugar for two minutes. Brush over the buns while they are still hot.

Simnel Cake: Le Simné

S imnel cake was made by the daughters of the house for their Mother on Mothering Sunday, the second Sunday in Lent. Now it seems to be associated only with Easter as this rich fruit cake is often decorated with eleven balls of marzipan representing the Apostles, the twelfth having already died.

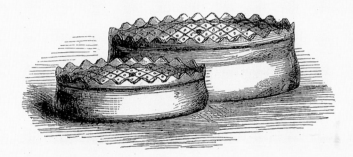

The name *simné* may have been derived from the old French word *simenel* meaning 'fine flour'. Originally, the cake was a saffron coloured pastry case, filled with dried fruits.

Quantities for a 22cm/9inch cake tin:

250g/8oz plain flour	120g/4oz currants
250g/8oz butter	120g/4oz raisins
250g/8oz soft brown sugar	120g/4oz glacé cherries
4 eggs	60g/2oz ground almonds
3 level tsp mixed spice	3 tbsp brandy
1 level tsp ground nutmeg	A good pinch of saffron threads
250g/8oz sultanas	

Marzipan

375g/12oz ground almonds
180g/6oz icing sugar
180g/8oz castor sugar
4 egg yolks
Half tsp almond essence
2 tbsp lemon juice

Line the tin with greased paper.

In a cup, cover the saffron threads with boiling water and in a large bowl soak the fruit in the brandy for at least one hour.

Meanwhile make the marzipan.

To make the marzipan, place the ingredients in the food processor. Process until all are well blended into a ball. Cut in half, wrapping one half in cling film.

To make the cake, cream the butter and sugar. Add the beaten eggs gradually.

Add the sifted flour and spices; then the fruit, ground almonds and finally the saffron water.

Place half the mixture in the tin. Shape half the marzipan into a flat disc the size of the tin and place over the mixture. Add the second half of cake mixture.

Bake at 165°C, 325°F, Gas 3 for one and a half to two hours, cover with foil if browning too much. Test to make sure it is cooked. Cool in the tin.

A day or so before eating, roll the second half of marzipan into a disc, cut out an inner circle. Spread a little jam on the outer edge of the cake then press the outer ring of marzipan on top. Use the inner circle of marzipan to make eleven balls. Make eleven indentations with a finger, place a little jam or egg white in each then gently press in each of the balls. Place the cake under a hot grill – or use a kitchen blow torch – to brown the marzipan and make it more attractive.

Before serving, remove the greaseproof paper and tie a ribbon around.

Pancakes or Crêpes with Orange Butter & Calvados

I mentioned pancakes at the beginning of Spring as a Lenten meal but of course they are delicious at any time of the year; if our grandchildren are anything to go by, it would be almost every day! So having introduced them in a savoury form, why not end with a flourish.

Using the same mixture as the Spinach Pancakes (see page 20) make the pancakes, piling them on to a plate: 14 cms/5.5 inches is a good size.

Orange Butter
For 6 people
2 oranges
250g/8oz butter
30g/1oz granulated sugar
3 tbsp Calvados or cognac

In the food processor, place the butter, sugar and finely grated orange peel. Very gradually pour in one tbsp Calvados and as much of the squeezed orange juice to make a thick cream. Scrape into a bowl and refrigerate. This can be done well in advance.

When finishing the crêpes, fold each in half and half again.

Place the orange butter in a roomy pan until it bubbles. Add the crêpes, spooning over the buttery sauce. Sprinkle them with two tbsp granulated sugar and the remaining liqueur.

Shake until thoroughly heated through. Serve with the syrup spooned over.

To flambé the crêpes, heat a further tablespoon of calvados or cognac, ignite and pour gently over the contents of the pan.

Pound Cake

This is an old recipe which has been in use for over two hundred years and is still just as good. This couldn't be an easier way of remembering a list of ingredients! Not only that, they make a perfect buttery, golden cake. All that is needed is:

1lb butter
1lb sugar
1lb self-raising flour
1 lb eggs - 8 eggs as an average egg weighs 2 oz
Now of course, it would be converted to 500g of everything.

There are variations such as added glacé cherries, walnuts or crystallised ginger.

The cake is made by creaming the butter and sugar. The beaten eggs are gradually added along with the sifted flour. It is baked in a greased and lined 9inch/23cms round tin and baked in a moderate oven 190°C, 375°F, Gas 5 for about forty-five minutes.

Well fortified, we blaze out of Spring and into Summer...

SUMMER

Jersey French	*été*
Guernsey French	*étaï* (m)

June ~ July ~ August

Summer is a busy time on the land and, before the advent of mechanisation, everybody lent a hand with haymaking.

Towards the end of summer came the harvesting of the cereal crops, principally wheat, barley and oats, which had been produced in the Islands since the Middle Ages. In the rural community, taxes were often paid in measures of wheat and properties were assessed accordingly. These 'wheat rentes', as they were known, could also be assessed in a monetary form. Old title deeds still testify to the practice. Up until the end of the nineteenth century the Islands were self sufficient in cereals and even exported surplus flour. Until the late 1800s there were numerous wind and water mills in the islands for grinding corn.

Bread is said to be the staff of life. In the islands it was known also as *tourte*. The better off could afford bread made from 'simnel', a fine white flour which was also the main ingredient for Simnel cakes. Nowadays, the health benefits of eating brown, wholemeal bread are well recognised.

Keeping bees was important for the bees' work in pollinating the orchards and plants and the added bonus of their honey. Honey is a product of the sun – it is the nectar from countless spring and summer flowers that is converted into high energy honey. Marie De Garis relates in her Folklore book that hives were often kept on the pig sty wall which gave the bees 'lift off'. Bees were part of family life and, if there was a death in the family, a piece of black crepe material would be tied around the hives as a mark of respect. Some believed that when a bee flies, a soul will rise to live again.

For most of us, Summer brings about something of a life-style change – we like to be outside as much as possible and our eating habits turn to picnics and possibly barbecues – fifty years ago we hadn't heard of these but, nowadays, who hasn't? In those days, eating outside was much more of a special occasion, often linked to a Sunday School outing or family picnic.

Summer also means salads – and salads mean tomatoes. Initially treated with suspicion when introduced from the New World, the tomato has become one of the most popular of fruits worldwide and, of course, has a particular association with the Channel Islands. The Jersey and Guernsey 'Tom' became the islands' most famous ambassador for much of the twentieth century. Marketing included the extraordinary claim that the humble tomato possessed aphrodisiac properties – it was known as the 'Love Apple'!

From the 1900s Jersey farmers found that, after lifting their early potatoes, they could produce successful outdoor tomato crops in the island's light sandy soil, thanks to the south-facing lie of the land. Soon, the fields of staked tomatoes bore a passing resemblance to the vineyards of France and Italy!

In Guernsey, tomatoes were initially raised in glass vine houses beneath the vines but, as tomatoes became increasingly profitable, the vines were removed. As a bonus, the local boat-building industry, which had been in decline, welcomed the work caused by the demand for the construction of tomato 'spans', as they were known.

Over the years, great ingenuity was used to maximise tomato production and, today, leading growers can achieve an average of 40lbs of fruit per plant!

Towards the end of the 1960s, outside factors led to a sharp decline in Channel Island tomato production, but it is well worth seeking out the locally grown product – a well grown Channel Island 'tom' beats any import!

Tomato

| Jersey French | *tonmate* (f) |
| Guernsey French | *tamate, toumate* (f) |

Tomato Salad

Tomato salad must be one of the most refreshing, appetising and colourful.

Simply slice them, then just before serving drizzle with a seasoned vinaigrette or simply olive oil, salt and ground black pepper. Scattered with torn mint or basil leaves; feta cheese gives added interest.

Tomato sauce

Made with fresh tomatoes, this sauce is really good hot or cold and goes with almost everything.

This will make about 275ml/10fl oz

750g/1.5lbs fresh tomatoes
1 good sized onion 200g/6oz
2 plump cloves garlic
3/4 sprigs thyme

1 red chilli
2-3 bay leaves
2 tbsp olive oil

In a saucepan or cast iron casserole, gently fry the roughly chopped garlic and onion in the oil for about five minutes. Add the chopped tomatoes, sprigs of thyme and chilli (unless you like a really hot sauce, remove the seeds). Season with ground black pepper. Cover with water add the bay leaves and simmer for a good hour.

Remove and discard the bay leaves. Either whizz in the food processor or pass through a mouli or sieve.

V
E
G
E
T
A
B
L
E
S

Cream of Tomato Soup

Serves 4
1 kilo/2lbs ripe tomatoes
1 onion
2 cloves garlic
2 celery stalks
2 medium potatoes (250g/8oz)
3/4 sprigs lemon thyme
150 ml/5fl oz cream
1 litre/40fl oz chicken or vegetable stock
30g/1oz butter
Chives for garnishing
Salt and pepper

Fry the chopped onion and garlic in the butter. Add the chopped tomatoes, celery stalks, thyme and potato. Add the stock and seasoning. Simmer for about an hour.

Either sieve or mouli the soup. Reheat, adding more stock if necessary. On serving, stir in the cream and scissor in a few chives.

Lettuce

Jersey French	*laitue* (f)
Guernsey French	*lettuche* (f)

Lettuce has been around for thousands of years and was introduced into Britain by the Romans. Over the years it has been improved so that there are many varieties and it has become our main salad plant. Lettuce can be the cabbage type with soft and pliable leaves, the crisp head with crispy leaves tightly packed or the long-leaved and loose-leaved lettuce which spreads openly and leaves cut as needed. A green salad is always popular, especially with a few leaves of rocket, some herbs or flowers such as nasturtium. Dressings should be added at the last minute otherwise the leaves will quickly become dark and limp.

Broad Beans

Jersey French	*fève* (f)
Guernsey French	*faïve* (f)

Broad beans are something to look forward to every summer. Often they are left too long on the plant before being picked so that they are past their prime and are tough and mealy to eat, often needing the outer skin of the bean to be removed.

Young broad beans as a salad or with parsley sauce are delicious. Baby ones can be picked when they are 5cms/ 2inches long and can be cooked and eaten in their pods.

~

Beans

Jersey	runner beans	*pais brantcheurs* (m pl)
French	French beans	*pais* (m pl), *d'mai, bâsinnièrs* (m pl) and *crapaûdins* (m pl)
Guernsey	runner bean	*graempaeux* (m)
French	French bean	*haricot* (m)

This is a large family descended from the common bean brought back from the New World by Spanish explorers ('french' beans are so called because of their longstanding popularity in France). They can be grown as dwarf, trailing or as runners trained up bamboo poles. French beans are delicious when picked green and young or can be allowed to mature and dry on the plant when they become 'haricots', the basis for our much loved bean jar or bean crock. Runner beans are, of course, eaten when young, in fact they become tough, stringy and unpleasant if left too long! Picking beans when young tends to encourage more to grow.

This is Nan du Feu's recipe for **un fricot d'pais d'mai** (a bean feast) – clearly, the quantities are flexible. Normally, freshly picked French beans and small freshly dug new potatoes are used although leftover boiled ones are acceptable.

Break (not slice) the beans into pieces and boil for about five minutes. Boil the potatoes until tender. While they are boiling, fry a few onions in butter or dripping. Add the beans and chopped potatoes, mix and fry for a few minutes.

V
E
G
E
T
A
B
L
E
S

Cucumber

Jersey French	*cocombre* (m)
Guernsey French	*coucaombre* (f)

My father was a tomato grower and I can remember at the end of a greenhouse or two, he would plant cucumbers. Like tomatoes, cucumbers are a vegetable that we children disliked. I think the reason was that the custom was to peel and slice them thinly and sprinkle them with salt, pepper and vinegar so that they became limp and sharp. There are many varieties and often the ones with a prickly skin have a better flavour.

A freshly sliced cucumber is crisp and refreshing. Cucumber mixes well with yoghurt and sour cream and also with tomatoes, spring onions and herbs such as dill, mint and parsley and spices such as ground coriander and cumin. Cucumber sandwiches remain popular especially during hot weather – they are refreshing with the cucumber giving added crunch.

Chilled Cucumber Soup

Serves 4
1 cucumber
275 ml/10fl oz plain yogurt
150ml/5fl oz double cream
1 clove garlic
2 tbsp olive oil
2 tbsp white wine vinegar
30g/1oz chopped toasted walnuts
1 tbsp chopped tarragon
Salt and pepper

Peel and finely dice the cucumber. Sprinkle with salt and leave for thirty minutes. Rinse and drain. Place everything except the walnuts in the blender or food processor. Whizz until smooth. Chill for two hours.

Spoon into individual bowl and sprinkle with the walnuts.

Cocombre à la Jèrriaise

This recipe is from Nan du Feu: Peel a cucumber and slice very thinly. Put in a bowl with a little salt. Shake and drain until all the juice has been extracted. Cover with vinegar and allow to stand for an hour or two then it is ready to eat with the **fricot d'pais d'mai** – bean feast.

Marrow/Courgettes

Jersey French	Courgette: *courgette* (f)
Guernsey French	Courgette: *courgeattes* (f)
	Marrow: *mouelle* (f)

Although any immature marrow may be called a courgette or zucchini, in recent years they have been bred to be dainty and small. There are many varieties in a range of greens and yellows.

The plants spread themselves, their large leaves protecting and concealing the fruit, so much so that often a courgette is missed, only to appear as a marrow. Their delicate flavour may be enhanced with herbs such as parsley and chives.

Courgettes with Tomatoes & Herbs

Serves 4
1 kilo/2lbs courgettes
3 medium tomatoes
1 tbsp chopped tarragon
120g/4oz butter
Salt and pepper

Finely slice the courgettes. Place a layer in an ovenproof casserole, sprinkle with the tarragon, the finely sliced tomatoes and half the butter. Season with salt and pepper. Add the remaining sliced courgettes, season and dot with the remaining butter. Bake in a moderate oven for about thirty minutes until crisp and golden.

VEGETABLES

V
E
G
E
T
A
B
L
E
S

Courgette Soufflé

Serves 6
Use a soufflé dish or any other oven-proof dish measuring approximately 18cm/7 inches.

500g/1lb courgettes
2 tbsp olive oil
60g/2oz butter and extra for buttering the dishes
60g/2oz plain flour
275ml/10fl oz milk
3 eggs
60g/2oz mature cheddar
Salt and pepper

Peel and slice the courgettes and fry in the oil in a saucepan until they have softened and absorbed the oil. Don't let them colour or let them stick to the bottom. This will take fifteen to twenty minutes.

Blend or mash to a smoothish consistency. Place in a bowl. Rinse the pan. Using the same pan, melt the butter, add the flour mixing until smooth. Gradually add the milk until it is smooth and thick, cook for about one minute. Season. Add the courgettes, egg yolks and cheese mixing well. Whisk the egg whites, gently folding them in.

Tip the mixture into a well buttered soufflé or ovenproof dish.

Bake at 190°C, 375°F, Gas 5 for thirty-five minutes. I like soufflés to be creamy inside, cook a little longer if you prefer them drier.

~

Peas

| Jersey French | *pais* (m) |
| Guernsey French | *peis* (m) |

Peas have been a staple food since ancient times. There are many varieties but the most familiar is the garden pea and, more recently, the snap pea which is eaten pod and all. Canned peas, though dull in colour, are very popular but have given way to the frozen pea. Frozen peas are very good as they are frozen within hours of being picked. Fresh peas, once picked, should be cooked as soon as possible as they quickly lose their flavour. This is why bought fresh peas are often disappointing. Having said that, there is nothing to beat freshly picked and cooked peas.

A good way of stretching them is to cook them with some finely cut julienne strips of carrot or finely shredded lettuce leaves. On serving, add chopped parsley and butter or cream. Dried peas make very good soups and broths, not forgetting pease pudding.

Garlic

| Jersey French | ail (m) |

A close relation to the onion but only in the last fifty years has it become indispensable in almost every household. It grows well in our climate; not as big as those from the hotter Continental countries but every bit as good.

Not only is it used in the kitchen but medicinally as well. Its curative effects for sore throats, coughs and colds and for purifying the blood are well known. A friend swears by chewing a clove of garlic to cure toothache. Garlic is also richer in minerals than other vegetables.

It has a powerful flavour and if crushed has an instantly recognisable smell.

Slivers of garlic inserted into lamb or a salad bowl rubbed with a clove or garlic mayonnaise are but a few of its many uses.

Mackerel

| Jersey French | *maqu'sé* (m) |
| Guernsey French | *macré, macreo, des makériaouts* or *macrillots* (m) |

What a welcome sight when we see the first silvery, smooth, blue-green, fork-tailed mackerel. Surely, they must be one of the most unique of all fish with their unusual dark markings and distinctive taste.

They have been part of islanders' lives for centuries and have been salted and exported from the Middle Ages until the sixteenth century. During the summer months they were a plentiful nutritious food, cheap too but, sadly, the 'penny mackerel' is a thing of the past.

Mackerel still hold their own not just because they have been a part of island life for so long but they contain so much that is good for us, especially in these health-conscious times.

Mackerel contains a high percentage of polyunsaturated oil (the good oils); their protein contains essential amino acids and they are a good source of vitamins A, B and D. Although mackerel live in salt water, they are low in salt and contain calcium, iron, phosphorous and other trace minerals. So you see they are a healthy option.

Mackerel goes well with sauces made from sour fruits such as rhubarb, lemon and gooseberries as the sharpness of any of them cuts the richness of its flesh.

Mackerel can be fried, baked, grilled or soused either filleted or whole. My favourite way is filleted, floured and fried, served with boiled new potatoes and a wedge of lemon.

Conger Eel

Jersey French	*andeguille* (f), *congre* (m)
Guernsey French	*congre* (m), *caongre* (m), *anguelle* (f)

F
I
S
H

Conger was once prolific throughout the islands but, like other fish, numbers have dwindled. Another reason that we don't see so much of it is because it is often used as bait.

In the past it was economically very important to islanders as it was salted and dried and exported as far away as Gascony.

This smooth, scaleless, serpent-like fish was, for locals, an inexpensive, nourishing food. One drawback is that it is very bony so care must be taken when eating it. The best cut is just behind the head.

The following recipe for Conger Soup was given to me by Eileen Le Sueur from Jersey. She assures me that you wouldn't know it was made with conger and, having tried out her recipe, I have to agree.

Conger Soup

Serves 6
The head and tail of a conger
1 small onion or 2 shallots
1 cupful of peas
A handful of parsley and thyme
1 small cabbage
1 litre/2 pints milk
Salt and pepper
Marigold petals

Wash the head and tail and place in a large pan. Cover with water, season with salt and pepper. Simmer for about an hour. You need about 20fl oz/1pint of stock.

Strain through a fine sieve, returning the stock to the pan. Add the milk, shredded cabbage, sliced onion and thyme. Simmer for about thirty minutes. Add the peas and simmer for a further ten minutes.

On serving, scatter with the chopped parsley and marigold petals.

F
I
S
H

Conger Pie

Serves 4
I kilo/2lb piece of neck end
  of conger
1 onion
250g/8oz mushrooms
120g/4oz piece of bacon
30g/1oz flour
60g/2oz butter
Salt and pepper

Flaky or Puff pastry for the lid. Alternatively mashed or sliced potato.

Remove the skin from the conger and as many bones as possible. Cut it into small chunks, at the same time searching for bones. Fry the chunks in butter until cooked. Remove from the pan and keep warm. In the same pan, fry the chopped bacon, then the sliced mushrooms and chopped onion then add the fried conger. Sprinkle with the flour, season and gently turn. Place in the pie dish. Add 275ml/10fl oz water.

Cover with the pastry, decorating it with the left over pieces. Brush with milk. If preferred cover with mashed or finely sliced potatoes.

Bake in a moderate oven 200°C, 400°F, Gas 6 for thirty minutes.

~

Monkfish

| Jersey French | *mouaine* (m) |
| Guernsey French | *violon* (m), *ange de mer* (f) or *rogne dé maïr* (f) |

Monkfish is a species that has gained popularity locally in the last few years, although it has always been lurking at the bottom of the sea. No doubt it was because there were so many other fish to choose from that the ugly monkfish was overlooked. It is now an expensive fish but worth every penny as it has a very good flavour and its texture is firm, so much so that it can be likened to scampi or lobster.

When buying monkfish, choose from a bigger tail as smaller ones can be disappointing.

Monkfish can take strong flavours such as ginger, bacon and anchovy.

Monkfish with Roasted Peppers

Serves 4
1 kilo/2lbs monkfish
2 red peppers
2 tbsp olive oil
30g/1oz butter

275ml/10fl oz fish stock
Pinch of saffron threads
1 tbsp red wine vinegar
Seasoning

Put the saffron threads and stock in a pan. Simmer until reduced by half. At the same time, roast or grill the peppers until charred and blistered. Put to one side and, when cool, remove the skin, core and seeds and cut into lengths.

Remove the membrane from the fish and cut into smallish chunks. Fry these in the olive oil until golden and tender. Remove from the pan and keep warm. Put the reduced liquor into the pan, adding the vinegar and butter in small pieces, whisking until well emulsified. Add the roasted peppers. Season.

Divide the monkfish and peppers between four plates. Pour the bubbling sauce over and around.

F
I
S
H

Roast Monkfish Tail

In France this dish is sometimes known as a 'gigot' because the shape of the tail resembles a leg of lamb and is cooked in a similar way.

Serves 4
1 kilo/2lb monkfish tail with
  the bone removed
2 cloves garlic
Sprigs of rosemary
3 shallots
150ml/5fl oz dry white wine
4 tbsp olive oil
Salt and pepper

Remove the membrane then insert slivers of garlic and spikes of rosemary down the two lengths. Place in a dish, pour over the wine, oil, add a few sprigs of rosemary, salt and freshly ground black pepper.

Marinate for at least two hours, spooning over the marinade every twenty minutes. If refrigerated, it can stay in the marinade for up to ten hours.

Fry the sliced shallots in a little oil and spread in an ovenproof dish. Lay the monkfish tail on top, pouring the juices over. Roast at 200°C, 400°F, Gas 6 for twenty to thirty minutes, basting occasionally.

Serve as it is with a white or hollandaise sauce, plus the addition of two tbsp chopped parsley and two tbsp chopped chives so that it is really green, a good contrast to the white meat.

~

John Dory

| Jersey French | Jean doré (m), dorée (f) |
| Guernsey French | Jean doraï (m) |

This is a common fish in Mediterranean waters but is also found further north and around the islands. Like the monkfish it is another ugly, spiky, skinny fish and difficult to fillet. It tends to be expensive as the flavour is particularly good.

The flesh is firm and the skin tough. All it needs in the way of cooking is to fry or grill the fillets and serve with a wedge of lemon. To prevent the fillet curling up during cooking, place the fillet, flesh down and make two diagonal cuts through the skin.

Lobster

Jersey French	honmard (m)
Guernsey French	houmard or houmar (m)
	houmarde (f) a hen

Lobsters are still abundant in our deep waters. They are a beautiful rich blue/black colour turning brick red on cooking. Lobsters are available all year round and are an ideal choice for outside eating. Lobster mayonnaise or lobster cooked under the grill or on the barbecue makes a meal extra special. It is easy to prepare as the body can be cut in half right through to the tail or the tail into segments. The uneven claws are easily cracked.

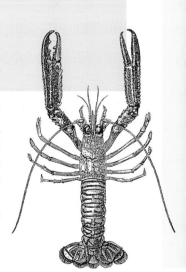

When it comes to picnics or taking food outside to feed hungry workers, keeping it simple is the name of the game. The ploughman's lunch is a good example – an unfussy yet nourishing meal. Nowadays the choice of food to take on picnics is huge but the good old sandwich remains the mainstay and the choice of fillings is enormous. Other foods such as pies, quiches and tarts are good but less easy to transport, though the advent of lidded containers makes it easier to carry all sorts of foods, whether sweet or savoury, on picnics.

Barbecues

Cooking outside, over wood or charcoal, is nothing new. Indeed, in the past it may often have been a necessity. However, barbecuing, as we now know it, has become immensely popular in recent years. Striking, exciting flavour can be imparted by the barbecue process and there is too the theatre of the occasion – an opportunity for the men to do their stuff!

The choice of equipment is vast – from the small, throwaway portables to refined gas-fired ones. Charcoal and wood have been replaced mainly by bricquettes and everlasting volcanic coals. Fish-shaped holders and grills come in many sizes too. Care must be taken when barbecuing as a tender fillet steak can soon become a cinder. Learning to judge the heat and adjust the cooking time to suit different foods is half the fun. Many fish and shellfish lend themselves to barbecueing. Here is one of my favourites.

Barbecued Mackerel

One of the best and simplest ways of cooking mackerel. You need one per person. Leave the head and tail on, simply wash and gut the fish. Place a good sized sprig of rosemary, sprigs of thyme or sage leaves in the belly cavity. Line one half of the fish-grill with bay leaves. Place the fish on top and cover with a second row of bay leaves. Close the grill and barbecue on a gentle heat for eight to ten minutes on both sides until the leaves are blackened or scorched. Pull the 'sacrificial' leaves away and the skin will come too, revealing the moist aromatic flesh.

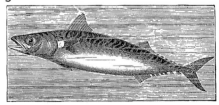

All meat can be barbecued but the humble burger must be a firm favourite.

Beefburgers

For 4 burgers, take 500g/ 1lb of good quality mince. Combine it with one egg, a dash of Worcestershire, salt and pepper. Divide into four and shape into a burger. Grill or barbecue approximately five minutes on each side. Crown with your favourite topping.

Brochettes

These are easily made and are ideal for barbecues as they cook easily and there is a varied choice of what you thread on them. Meat such as pork, beef, lamb, chicken which has been marinated in a favourite sauce can be used, interspersed with cherry tomatoes, onion, mushroom or sliced peppers. If using wooden brochette sticks remember to soak in cold water or they will burn.

Char-grilled Vegetables

These are always popular. Blistered peppers, corn on the cob, courgettes, tomatoes and onions all taste better from the barbecue. Par boiled potatoes finished off on the grill then split and filled with butter and chopped chives or other fillings are essential.

Garlic Bread

This is quick and easily made and can be prepared well in advance, even frozen.

For two Baguettes
250g/8oz salted butter
6 fat cloves garlic, peeled and chopped
4 tbsp olive oil
4 tbsp of chopped parsley.

Whizz the butter and garlic. Gradually add the oil until well blended. Add the parsley just using the pulse switch. Season with ground black pepper. Scrape the butter out and chill. Spread the baguettes generously, roll in foil and bake for about fifteen minutes in a hot oven or on the barbecue.

Salads

| Jersey French | Salade (f) |
| Guernsey French | Salade (f) |

The choice is huge. Most salads should be quickly and freshly made otherwise they become limp and soggy. Vinaigrettes should normally be added at the last moment. Here are a few ideas, each salad being enough for four people.

Green Salad with Bacon & Croutons

In a large salad bowl, mix about twelve rocket leaves and one lettuce or the equivalent amount of salad leaves. Sprinkle with thin strips of cooked streaky bacon and garlicky croûtons. Dress with a lemon vinaigrette and scatter with nasturtium or marigold petals and a scissoring of chives.

Potato Salad

Slice 1 kilo/2lbs freshly boiled warm potatoes in a bowl. Scatter with fried onion and bacon pieces. Add one tbsp chopped parsley and a chopped hard boiled egg. Dress with a mustardy vinaigrette.

Broad Bean & Lemon Salad

500g/1lb cooked broad beans with a generous amount of chopped herbs, the juice of half a lemon, a swirl of olive oil, salt and freshly ground black pepper.

French Bean Salad

Put 750g/1.5lbs cooked French beans, while still hot, in a salad bowl. Add a generous combination of fresh herbs such as parsley, coriander, chives, tarragon, etc., chopped or torn. Drench with a mustardy vinaigrette. Turn and leave to cool.

Mushroom Salad

Wash 500g/1lb mushrooms and slice into a salad bowl. Drizzle with 2 tbsp olive oil and the juice from one lemon. Season with ground pepper and turn gently. Leave. Before serving, add some more oil, and a sprinkle of salt. Turn gently once more and place on a bed of shredded lettuce. Garnish with chopped parsley and chives.

Cucumber & Yogurt Salad

Peel a cucumber. Cut in half lengthways. If you feel it is necessary, remove the seeds. Dice the cucumber. Spoon over natural yoghourt, 3-4 tbsp olive oil, one level tsp ground cumin, chopped mint, salt and ground black pepper. Mix and chill before serving.

Courgette, Tomato & Tarragon Salad

Finely slice about 750g/1.5lbs of courgettes. Fry gently in olive oil followed by three or four sliced tomatoes. Add a scattering of ground coriander and cumin. Put in a salad bowl. Finely slice a couple of spring onions and add them. Squeeze the juice of half a lemon, scatter with tarragon leaves, season with salt and ground black pepper.

Watercress

Jersey French	*cresson* (m)
Guernsey French	*d'la bête* (f)

Watercress used to be much more common and popular. I well remember people picking it in the stream below our house. Their hands would be blue with cold as they worked in their wellies in the well-tended beds. The beds are no longer there but if you see watercress growing wild do try some if you are happy that the stream is not polluted. Watercress makes a fiery salad and an excellent soup.

Watercress Salad

Take two bunches of watercress. Remove most of the stalks. Put in a salad bowl and add two cooked beetroot that have been sliced and cut into julienne strips. In a small bowl mix one tbsp horseradish sauce with one tbsp wine vinegar, two tbsp olive oil, salt and pepper. Mix well and just before serving, coat the watercress and beetroot.

Raspberries

| Jersey French | *frambouaise* (f) |
| Guernsey French | *frànbouaise* |

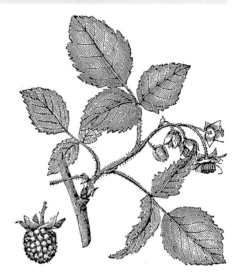

Raspberries must be the most delicious of the soft fruits. Their flavour is reliable, unlike strawberries which can be disappointing or loganberries which can be very sour.

They never become big and blowzy but remain delicate with a soft bloom. They are easy to grow, bearing fruit from July, with some varieties fruiting into early autumn.

I think it is a pity to do anything with raspberries except enjoy them whole with sugar and cream or ice cream but here are a few ideas.

Old Fashioned Raspberry Sponge Flan

I remember my Mother used to make sponge flans which were filled with different fruits including tinned mandarin oranges. Her sponge was really a genoese mixture as she found it didn't dry out so quickly. Whatever the fruit, the flan was covered with jelly and served with a jug of cream. They were delicious with no effort involved in eating as they just slipped down. The sponge tin had a lip or rim so that the cooked sponge had a wall keeping in the fruit but in particular the jelly. It is worth buying a silicone lined sponge tin as this helps to avoid the disappointment when part of the rim doesn't come out.

A flan of 8 average servings:

Sponge	Filling
90g/3oz plain flour	500g/1lb raspberries
90g/3oz castor sugar	275ml/10fl oz redcurrant or raspberry jelly
2 eggs	2/3 tbsp sweet sherry (optional)
30g/1oz melted	150ml/5fl oz cream or crème fraîche
unsaltedbutter	1 packet raspberry jelly

Use a silicone-coated sponge flan tin. The instructions say that it isn't necessary to butter the tin but I am not prepared to risk disaster! So to be on the safe side, I butter and flour mine.

I suggest making the raspberry jelly first so that it can cool and begin to set. Make it according to the instructions on the packet. You will need approximately 275ml/10fl oz.

Put the eggs and sugar in a bowl, placing it over a pan of simmering water. Whisk until thick and creamy. Add the melted butter. Remove the bowl from the pan, allow to cool a little before folding in the sieved flour. Spoon into the flan tin and bake at 180°C, 350°F, Gas 4 for twenty to thirty minutes. Turn out and cool on a wire rack.

Sprinkle the base of the sponge with sherry. Spread a layer of whisked cream or the crème fraîche over the base of the sponge. Arrange the raspberries, then chill for thirty minutes. This will help the jelly to set as it should be just on the point of setting when you spoon it over the fruit. Serve with a pouring cream.

Raspberry Ripple

2 punnets of raspberries (or strawberries)
140ml/4fl oz double cream
125g/4oz good plain chocolate
1 tbsp castor sugar
1 tbsp sweet sherry
Sprigs of mint

Pour the cream and sugar in a bowl. Whisk until soft and creamy. Fold the sherry into the mixture. Grate the chocolate on the coarse grater.

Take four glasses. Layer the cream, raspberries and chocolate twice. Chill and just before serving decorate with sprigs of mint.

F
R
U
I
T

Raspberry Tartlets

This is a good way of eking out raspberries.
You will need up to about two punnets which
is sufficient to make at least eight tartlets
plus 150ml/5fl oz double cream.

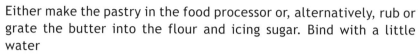

Sweet Shortcrust Pastry
180g/6oz flour
120g/4oz butter
30g/1oz icing sugar
150ml/5fl oz
Either make the pastry in the food processor or, alternatively, rub or
grate the butter into the flour and icing sugar. Bind with a little
water
Line patty tins with the pastry. Bake in a moderate oven. When cool,
fill with whipped double cream, piling raspberries on top

Alternatively bake a shortcrust pastry case filling it in the same way.

Instead of cream, crème pâtissière may be used which can be made
in advance.

Crème Pâtissière
275ml/10fl oz double cream
3 egg yolks
1 tsp cornflour
60g/2oz sugar
In a roomy bowl, beat the egg yolks, cornflour and sugar. Heat the
cream to almost boiling point then gently and gradually add to the
egg mixture. On a very low heat, stirring all the time, bring the
mixture very slowly to almost boiling point but don't let it boil or it
will curdle. Once thick, remove from the heat and, stirring
occasionally, let it cool, then refrigerate. When cold, spoon into the
pastry cases. Arrange the raspberries on top. If you like, you can
glaze the top with redcurrant jelly.

~

Summer Pudding

This is a favourite as I love the way the juice from the fruit soaks into the bread. It is normally made in a pudding basin.

Serves 6
Mixed fruit weighing up to about 750g/1.5lbs of mainly raspberries and redcurrants but some blackcurrants, strawberries and logan-berries can be used.
120g/4oz sugar
6-8 slices or 120g/4oz of white bread, crusts removed.

Clean and rinse the fruit. Put in a pan with the sugar and heat until the juice runs and the sugar dissolves. Two or three tbsp water may be needed to help get it going. Add more sugar if you don't find the fruit sweet enough. When soft, drain through a sieve so that the juice runs into a bowl.

Cut the bread into fingers. Dip each piece into the fruit juice, overlapping them as you work around the basin. Cut a circle of bread to fit snugly in the bottom. Carefully spoon the softened fruit into the lined basin. Add sufficient juice almost covering the fruit. The bread will absorb the juice. Cover with a lid of bread. Place a plate on top that fits within the rim. Weigh it down with something heavy so that the pudding compacts down.

Refrigerate overnight. Run a knife around the basin. Place a plate on top, turn out the pudding and serve with cream or crème fraîche.

~

F
R
U
I
T

Strawberries

Jersey French	*frâse* (f)
Guernsey French	*frâse* (f)

Strawberries – one of summer's luxuries.

Strawberry Fool

Fools are easy to make. They can be made with many fruits either mashed or puréed. It depends whether you prefer a lumpy or smooth consistency.

Serves 4
500g/1lb strawberries
275ml/10fl oz double cream
120g/3oz castor sugar
1 tbsp grated dark chocolate

Mash or purée the strawberries reserving four small ones for decoration. Add the sugar. Whip the cream until soft. Fold in the sugared mashed or puréed strawberries. Spoon into individual glasses. Decorate with the reserved strawberries and a grating of plain chocolate.

Strawberry Meringue or Pavlova

Meringues are drier than Pavlovas which have a crisp outer shell and softer centre.

Serves 6
Meringue
3 egg whites
180g/6oz castor sugar

Filling
275 ml/10fl oz double cream
500g/1lb strawberries

Pavlova
3 egg whites
180g/6oz castor sugar
1.5 tsp white wine vinegar
Half tsp vanilla essence

Heat the oven at 150°C, 300°F, Gas 2.

Take a piece of non-stick silicone paper. Draw a circle about 21 cm/ 8 inches and place the whole sheet on a baking tray.

With an electric mixer, whisk the egg whites until stiff. Whisk in two thirds of the sugar. Fold in the remainder by hand.

If you are making the Pavlova, now fold in the vinegar and vanilla essence. For both, spoon the mixture onto the circle shaping it into a nest.

Bake the Pavlova for about forty-five minutes. Once cooked turn off the oven and leave until it is easy enough to handle so that the paper can be removed.

Bake the Meringue for two to three hours until it is dry and the paper can be peeled off.

Fill with softly whipped cream and strawberries.

Loganberries

Guernsey French   *fràncmaeure* (f)

Tart describes them – I don't think I have ever tasted one that is meltingly sweet. They need lots of sugar and cream and make one of the most delicious jams.

They can be used in the same way as raspberries but remember extra sugar!

F
R
U
I
T

Gooseberries

| Jersey French | *grouaîsile* (f) |
| Guernsey French | *quérouaiseau* (m) |

Gooseberry bushes are hardy, happily surviving our south-westerlies. 'Goosegogs', as we call them, range from green to yellow or deep red in colour and they can be smooth or hairy. Gooseberries can be used to make pies, fools, jam, sauce or just plain stewed. The tartness of the gooseberry can counteract the richness of fish such as mackerel or herring.

Over the years, the gooseberry has suffered neglect which is a pity. One reason could be that it ripens at the same time as all the soft fruit and as a result loses out.

It is interesting to note that we use it mainly in sweet dishes whereas across the water in France it is mainly used in savoury dishes.

Honeyed Gooseberries & Elderflower

Serves 4
750g/1.5lbs gooseberries topped and tailed
2 handfuls of elderflower heads – open ones if possible as they are more fragrant. If you can't find any, use 3 tbps elderflower syrup
3 tbsp runny honey
150ml/5fl oz water

In an ovenproof dish or enamel lined saucepan (not aluminium), put all the ingredients. Simmer gently or cook in a moderate oven until the gooseberries have collapsed. Cool and when cold take out the elderflower heads.
Serve with double cream, crème fraîche or ice-cream.

Gooseberry Fool

Serves 4
500g/1lb gooseberries
60g/2oz butter
4 tbsp soft brown sugar
250ml/10fl oz double cream
Grated nutmeg
A little cream and toasted chopped hazelnuts for decoration

Gently stew the gooseberries with the grated nutmeg, butter and sugar for about fifteen minutes until they have collapsed. Press through a nylon sieve and allow the purée to cool. Whip the cream until softly thick, then fold it into the purée. Spoon into four glasses and decorate. Chill for at least three hours. Serve with tiny macaroons (see page 185).

Gooseberry Pudding

Serves 4
750g/1.5lbs gooseberries – topped and tailed
150g/5oz butter
150g/5oz castor sugar
180g/6oz self-raising flour
3 eggs
60g/2oz granulated sugar
3 or 4 pieces of ginger preserved in syrup

Cream the butter and castor sugar until soft and fluffy. Add the beaten eggs one at a time. Fold in the self-raising flour.

Put the gooseberries in a pie dish adding three or four tbsp water. Sprinkle with sugar and chopped pieces of ginger. Spoon the mixture over.

Bake for thirty to forty minutes at 190°C, 375°F, Gas 5

Gooseberry Mint Jelly
See Preserves, page 152

F
R
U
I
T

Blackcurrants

| Jersey French | *néthes gradiles* (f pl) |
| Guernsey French | *nère gradille* (f) |

Blackcurrants have long been appreciated not only in the kitchen but for their use as a syrup to cure sore throats. At the beginning of the twentieth century their popularity was boosted when their high percentage of Vitamin C was discovered – who hasn't heard of Ribena!

Blackcurrants go well with other fruits such as apples and pears.

Blackcurrant Flummery

Serves 4
500g/1lb blackcurrants
15g/half oz cornflour
1 orange
120g/4oz granulated sugar
4 tbsp double cream
1 tbsp Kirsch

Pare an orange slicing the peel into thin strips. Put on a tray in a cool oven to dry out.

Put the blackcurrants in a pan with 150ml/5fl oz water. Add the squeezed orange juice and sugar. Simmer gently until cooked. Pass through a fine sieve. Dissolve the cornflour in a little water. Add to the blackcurrants, bring gently to the boil, boil for two minutes. Remove from the heat, stir in the kirsch, when cool enough, pour into four glasses. Refrigerate. On serving, pour one tbsp of cream on each and scatter some of the dried orange peel on top.

Damsons and plums may be used in the same way.

Peaches

Jersey French	*pêche* (f)
Guernsey French	*pêche* (f)

They have long been grown in the islands, either under glass or in sheltered sunny corners. There is something very special about the velvety skin, almost downy, and its luscious juiciness and firm flesh.

Nectarines are of the same family with a glossy skin and firm flesh. Their juice has a particularly fine flavour, so much so that in ancient times it was known as 'nectar of the Gods'.

Sliced skinned peaches sprinkled with sugar and cognac and marinated for a few hours is one of the best ways of enjoying this fruit.

Baked Stuffed Peaches/ Nectarines

Peaches and nectarines are interchangeable for this recipe which offers something a little different when there is a glut.

Serves 8
8 ripe peaches or nectarines
2 egg whites
120g/4oz castor sugar
120g/4oz ground almonds
1 tsp almond essence
6 tbsp port or madeira

Whisk the egg whites. Fold in the sugar, ground almonds and essence. Cut the fruit in half. Remove the stones. Fill the cavities with the mixture. Bake at 180°C, 350°F, Gas 4 for twenty minutes. Spoon over the port or Madeira and cook for a further fifteen minutes. Serve warm or cold with cream.

F
R
U
I
T

Plums

| Jersey French | *preune* (f) |
| Guernsey French | *preune* (f) |

Plums and Damsons can be difficult to grow but, with care taken over feeding and watering, they can do well. In Spring their young buds are a great attraction to birds. I remember a plum tree espaliered against the house where I was brought up which was full of fruit year after year.

Plum Fool

Serves 4
500g/1lbs ripe plums
2 tsp gelatine
120g/4oz sugar
250ml/10fl oz double cream
1 tsp powdered cinnamon

Stone the plums. Put them in a pan with the sugar, cinnamon and a little water. Cover and simmer until cooked. Cool and sieve them. Sprinkle the gelatine on three tbsp warm water, place in a pan or bowl of hot water, stirring now and again until dissolved. Stir the gelatine into the plum purée. Whip the cream until fairly thick, stir in the plum purée. Spoon into four glasses and chill until set. Decorate with toasted flaked almonds.

Battered Plum Pudding

Serves 4
750g/ 1.5 lbs ripe plums
60g/2oz plain flour
90g/3oz sugar
2 eggs
150ml/5fl oz single cream
30g/1oz melted butter
1 tsp almond essence
60g/2oz flaked almonds

Halve the plums, removing the stone. Layer the plums in an ovenproof casserole.

To make the batter, place the flour in one bowl and the eggs in another. Lightly whisk the eggs, then mix in the melted butter, cream, almond essence and sugar. Combine these ingredients with the flour and whisk until thoroughly mixed, then pour over the plums and scatter with flaked almonds.

Bake at 180°C, 350°F, Gas 4 for about forty-five minutes.

Plum Crunch

Serves 4

750g/1.5lbs plums
120g/4oz sugar
60g/2oz porridge oats

60g/2oz flour
1 tsp cinnamon
60g/2oz butter

Halve the plums, remove the stones and put in an ovenproof pie dish. Sprinkle with half the sugar and two tbsp water. In a bowl grate the butter into the flour and cinnamon. Add the porridge oats and remaining sugar. Scatter over the plums.

Cook at 180°C, 350°F, Gas 4 for forty-five minutes. Serve with cream or custard.

F
R
U
I
T

Plum Pudding

Serves 4

750g/1.5lbs ripe plums
2 eggs
120g/4oz self-raising flour

90g/3oz castor sugar
90g/3oz butter
1 tsp almond essence

Cream the butter and sugar. Add the beaten eggs, fold in the flour and almond essence. If necessary, add a little mix for a soft consistency. Spoon over the plums and bake at 180°, 350°, Gas 4 for approximately forty-five minutes.

Serve with warm cream or crème fraîche.

Plum & Almond Tart

Serves 6

Pastry
180g/6oz plain flour
120g/4oz butter
2 tbsp water

Filling
90g/3oz butter
90g/3oz sugar
90g/3oz ground almonds
2 eggs
1 tsp almond essence
1 kilo/2lbs plums

Make the pastry in a food processor. Alternatively rub or grate in the butter, mixing with a little water. Line a 20cm/8inch tin with the pastry.

In the food processor, whizz the butter, sugar and eggs. Add the ground almonds and essence. Spoon into the pastry case. Halve the plums removing the stone. Place in circles on the mixture - they will bury themselves as they cook. Bake at 190°C, 375°F, Gas 5 for about thirty to forty minutes.

Grapes

Jersey French	*vèrjus* (m) *nièr*	black grape
	vèrjus (m) *blianc*	white grape
Guernsey French	*nère grappe* (f)	black grape
	bllànche grappe	white grape

Our dessert grapes have always been and remain highly prized. Growing under glass protects them from the elements and care and attention results in excellent quality.

Black Hamburgh is the most widely known and best quality black dessert variety. The dessert white Muscat grape is juicy yet the flesh is firm with a good musky flavour. The family of Muscat grapes includes the Cannon Hall, Muscat of Alexandria and White Frontignon; for most people the Cannon Hall is considered the superior variety.

Locally grown grapes are in a class of their own and should be enjoyed as they are with no other adornment.

F
R
U
I
T

Melons

Jersey French	m'lon (m)
Guernsey French	mélaon (m)

Melons were first raised under glass in the early 1800s in Guernsey. I remember being shown a photograph, taken in 1900, by my late cousin Peter Falla whose Grandfather, Alfred Corbet, was known as the Melon King. Hundreds of round melons hung from plants that had been trained up cords, over wires and down the other side. It was a wonderful sight. These melons were exported to England.

The popular melons were from the Canteloup and Netted families but large-scale production of melons has long since ceased. However, some are still grown locally and if you spot one, do buy it – you won't regret it! It may be better not to chill melon before eating as this does not necessarily improve the delicate flavour; in other words, try it at room temperature.

Here are a few ideas for using melon. Melon and ginger is a well known combination – the ginger may be either powdered or crystallised. Melon chunks accompanied by soft fruits such as raspberries or strawberries is another way. Or perhaps a medley of different coloured melon chunks sprinkled with lemon juice and a scattering of shredded mint leaves. Melon slices are a traditional partner for Parma ham or prosciutto.

EIGHTH MONTH — AUGUST — THIRTY-ONE DAYS

Figs

Jersey French	*figue* (f)
Guernsey French	*figue* (f)

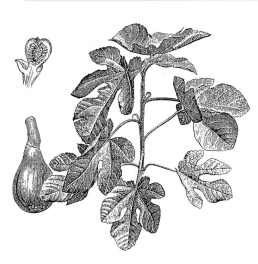

Figs grow extremely well throughout the islands under glass and even outside. Invariably a fig tree was found beside a pig-sty giving shade to the occupants who in turn gave nourishment to the tree. Figs were so eagerly awaited that I have seen a fig-tree full of small brown paper bags. Each contained a fig, the bag having been tied securely to fend off birds, wasps and other intruders. I have a friend who still does this every year. Of course freshly picked figs are a treat worth waiting for.

Sliced figs may be used as an accompaniment to cold meat such as Parma ham and slices of smoked duck.

Baked Figs

Serves 4

8 plump figs
3 tbsp runny honey
Juice of 1 lemon
Ground cinnamon

Sit figs in an ovenproof dish, drizzle with honey and lemon juice and dust with ground cinnamon. Cook in a moderate oven for twenty minutes. Cool, serve with crème fraîche.

F
R
U
I
T

Fresh Fig & Lemon Tart

Serves 6 to 8
Pastry
120g/4oz butter
180g/6oz flour

Filling

Make the lemon curd (see page 190) using two lemons, 60g/2oz butter,
  2 eggs and 180g/6oz sugar
Approximately eight to ten figs depending on size
1 tsp fennel seeds
1 level tbsp Demerara sugar

Make the pastry in the usual way by rubbing in the butter and adding
a little water to bind it. Alternatively, make it in the food precessor.
Line a 20cm/8inch flan dish. Spoon in a layer of lemon curd. Finely
slice the figs and radiate them overlapping around the dish until it
is filled. Scatter with demerara sugar and fennel seed. Bake at 180°C,
350°F, Gas 4 for forty-five minutes. When cool, serve with cream
whisked to a soft consistency.

AUTUMN

Jersey French	*automne*
Guernsey French	*autaomme* (m)

September ~ October ~ November

Autumn, a time for getting ready for winter. And we are reminded as we take and plant cuttings and gather seeds that we are also preparing for next year. Leaves turn from green through the autumnal shades until they begin to fall. Like the leaves, we are gently eased from the long bright days of summer into shorter days and a drop in temperature until, by November, the trees are bare and it is cold. Reluctantly, summer things have been put away. Gardens, hedges and fields are cut back and cleared of dead or dying vegetation. Many birds migrate to warmer climes. Animals grow thicker coats and we too bring out our winter woollies.

The main harvest from the land is during Autumn and it is the time when Church services take place to celebrate with gratitude the earth's bounty. I can remember my Grandmother used to save all her very best bunches of black grape to be tied on the altar rail on Harvest Sunday. Woe betide any of us pinching even one grape!

Some animals gather food to see them through the winter and many of us make preparations by making jams and chutneys, bottling and pickling various fruits and vegetables. Our diet changes. Gone are the summer delights, so easy to prepare. It is time for more robust meals.

The land must be fed in readiness for new crops. One very important fertiliser is seaweed – *vraic* – and now is the time to gather it. It was used in great quantities for spreading on fields and gardens. But horticultural and agricultural methods have changed over the years and, with the decline in both industries, the use of *vraic* has now virtually ceased in Guernsey, apart from a few die-hard amateurs. In Jersey, however, some potato growers still use *vraic*, albeit collected by mechanical means. So this abundant, valuable, organic natural resource lies largely neglected on our back doorstep.

I should like to include an anecdote from Nan Du Feu who tells the story that when she was living in Cornwall she covered her front garden with seaweed. Local farmers told her that she was making a big mistake and that everything in the garden would be destroyed by the salt in the seaweed. In trepidation she waited for Spring to come. The farmers were wrong and she had a magnificent display of tulips, so much so that one visitor was heard to say that it looked like a miniature Holland.

In the past, seaweed was also dried and used as fuel for fires in the home. It must have given off a strong smell as it burned but it was plentiful and free. No doubt, like all things, it was something you got used to. It was also burnt to produce potash as this is a good plant food. There was a constant demand for the "ash" and many people living on the coast would have fires continually burning for this purpose.

Gathering vraic was an annual ritual, back-breakingly hard and often dangerous work but it had its lighter moments. Some of the younger ones would gather on the beach looking for winkles and limpets which they would cook on the spot. The women, especially in Jersey, baked galettes à vrai – which are traditional large currant or raisin buns brought to the beach to satisfy ravenous appetites.

The apple has been very much part of island life. Around the 1500s the appearance of the islands was beginning to change with apple orchards being planted around farms. Cider was made to satisfy the needs of the family but slowly the industry grew until there was enough to be exported.

Conversely, apples were imported when the islands couldn't produce enough for cider-making. Not only were apples imported from Normandy but cider as well. And the cider continued its journey to England without duties being paid! The French, who for centuries disliked the English and didn't like to trade with them directly, would happily do so this way.

Cider making started in October, finishing in January. The apples were crushed in round granite troughs by a horse hitched to a huge granite wheel. The pulp would then be taken to the press where it would be spread between layers of straw. A huge screw pressed down the layers, the resulting juice would pass through a sieve into storage tubs before being decanted into barrels. Fermentation would then take place lasting two to three weeks and during that time any scum rising to the surface would be removed through a bung hole at the top. Bottling would then take place, making sure that the cider would be ready for the festive season.

We still see old apple crushers used as garden ornaments. However, in Guernsey, a company has recently been established using locally grown apples to produce an excellent Rocqette cider. In Jersey, La Mare Vineyards also produce cider, including a sparkling variety called *pompette* which means merry.

Another autumnal activity on many properties in Jersey was the annual preparation of black butter – a concentrated spread made from the slow cooking of large quantities of apples. It was an occasion for the family to gather to help stoke the fire and continue the stirring over two days and nights. When ready, the black butter was stored in crocks to be used throughout the year. The tradition is kept alive by enthusiastic groups and continues to be a jolly occasion.

Autumn heralds the beginning of the game season and the occasional sound of shotguns is a reminder that rabbits are being hunted. Much shellfish will be at its best while fish such as skate, black bream and pollack/whiting are also very good.

With the festive season in mind, animals and poultry are being fattened for slaughter. Pigs were the first to be killed. Pork was the most widely used meat and would last a family many months. As a result, practically every farm and smallholder kept pigs.

October and November were the months to call the pig killer – *le tuaeux d'pourchiaöux*. According to Marie De Garis' book on Folklore, it was important to call him at the right time otherwise the meat might become tainted. Killing should take place when the moon is waxing, never when it is waning. She also mentions the fact that pig-killers were very good bonesetters as the pig's bone structure is similar to ours.

As a twelve year-old, I can vividly remember a visit to our house by the pig killer. He was a big strong man and needed to be, because the pig waiting to meet its end weighed around 300 pounds. The unfortunate animal first had to be dragged to the spot in our back yard where a table had been set up and other equipment arranged. There, the pig killer, straddling the desperate animal and using a brawny arm to apply a head hold, despatched it with a quick slice of the throat. The spurting blood was caught in a half barrel where it was stirred with a stick, soon congealing into a shiny, crimson, jelly-like mass. The dead pig was then hung by its hind trotters from a convenient branch of a tree or sturdy beam so that it could be emptied, cleaned and the skin scraped.

Next the animal was laid on the table ready for cutting up but, before the butchering started, the men decided to have a tea break, leaving me staring atthe corpse of what had been, until a few moments ago, almost a family pet!

Suddenly, to my horror, the carcass started to move and slid with a thud onto the ground! Imagining the poor animal was coming back to life, I fled in terror, unaware that the incident was due simply to the unevenness of the yard where the table was standing!

Tea break over, the pig was cut up. I can't remember how our pig was disposed of but my brother tells me that some cuts were heavily salted; this process drew out moisture and, once drained, the meat would be stored in crocks of brine. Jim de Garis tells me he recalls that salt was rubbed on the skin but patted on the underside or flesh and that pepper was rubbed into the 'ball' joints. The meat was then hung in a barn to drain before being cut up and sold, stored in crocks of brine or dried on racks in the kitchen.

A lovely story from Marie De Garis' Folklore book describes that, at the time of killing a pig, a ham was often kept *pour si en cas* – just in case. A smoked ham was wrapped in a white cloth and placed on *les lattes d'pourchiaöux* – the rack in the kitchen. Should anyone in the family die, after the service the funeral party would do *le r'tour*, meaning returning to the house. The ham had been taken down and made ready to eat. Hence the saying *mangier son jàmbaon* (eating his ham). At the same time, a place at the table with an empty chair would be kept for the dead man.

One of the most basic Channel Islands' staples is bean jar or bean crock and as this is generally made with pig's trotters or a hock, what better recipe to start with?

Pig

Bean Jar or Bean Crock

Jersey French	un Piot et des Pais au Fou
Guernsey French	enne Jarraïe d'Harïcaots

This simple dish depends for success on long slow cooking, usually overnight. Reflecting humble origins, bean jar or crock remains a very economical meal to make. Now, it is accorded some sort of national status by virtue of its heritage. It can also be very good to eat as well as being satisfying.

The basis is haricot beans and pork on the bone. Some prefer a mixture of beans such as haricots and butter beans. Pigs' trotters are a very traditional ingredient. A hock can also be used, smoked or not – the important thing is for the meat to be on the bone to get a rich gravy which gels on cooling. Sometimes a shin of beef is used instead of pork. The other ingredients are an onion or two, bay leaves, salt, pepper and water.

Right up until the end of the Occupation bean jars, covered with brown paper and tied with string and with the owner's name on a label, were very often carried in a bucket to a bakery to cook overnight. A modest charge of a penny would be made.

On just such an occasion, a friend of ours, then a young boy, was entrusted with collecting the family bean jar from a bakery in Victoria Road, St Peter Port. On the way home, the precious bean jar fell. Not only was the jar smashed

M
E
A
T

but the meal was lost too. This was a major disaster as it was still war time and food was very scarce.

Bean Jar or Crock was often dished up for Sunday morning breakfast. Another breakfast dish was slices of pickled pork cooked in an oven. Pieces of bread were placed in the bottom of the oven which would toast at the same time, catching the dripping from the bacon.

Serves 6
500g/1lb haricot beans
Piece of leg pork on the bone weighing about 750g/1lb 8ozs
Alternatively one pig's trotter with some extra pork as there isn't
   much meat on a trotter
2 large onions
3-4 bay leaves
Salt and pepper

Soak the haricot beans in cold water overnight or for about twelve hours until they have swollen. Rinse them and place in an earthenware bean jar or crock. If you don't have time or have forgotten to soak the beans, cover them with water and bring slowly to the boil. Leave to cool in the water for an hour. Rinse and put in the bean jar. Push the meat in amongst the beans. Add the quartered onions, bay leaves and pepper.

Cover and cook gently in a moderate oven for at least five hours, even overnight but make sure the oven isn't too hot. Check occasionally to make sure there is enough liquid. Nearing the end of cooking, season with salt.

Roast Pork

Most of us find the crackling of roast pork irresistible - but how is good crackling achieved?

Rinse the joint under cold water. Next, at 1 cm/half inch intervals, cut or score the surface of the skin to get a ribbed effect. Rub the surface with oil and a good sprinkling of salt. Roast at thirty-five minutes to every 500g/1lb of meat. Start in a hot oven 215°C, 425°F, Gas 7 for the first thirty minutes until the crackling looks crisp and golden, then reduce the heat to 190°C, 375°F, Gas 5.

A de-boned piece of pork will take less time to cook than a joint on the bone. When cooking pork, always make sure it is well done.

Another way of producing crackling is to entirely remove the skin, lay it flat scoring it carefully, trying to keep it in one piece. Sprinkle with salt and roast in a very hot oven for about thirty minutes. Cooking it this way, the whole of the skin turns into crackling whereas roasting it on the joint means the underneath skin can remain tough and leathery.

M
E
A
T

Pork Chops with Cider

Serves 4

4 plump chops
275 ml / 10 fl oz cider
1 large onion
3-4 leaves sage

1 level tablespoon plain flour
Salt and pepper
30g/1oz butter or lard

Brush the chops with a little lard or butter. Cook under the grill for about ten minutes on each side depending on the thickness. Alternatively, cook them in a hot oven for fifteen to twenty minutes, turning once. Remove from the pan and keep warm. Cook the sliced onion in the juicy fat from the chops until soft. Sprinkle with the flour, add the chopped sage leaves and cider. Gently bring to the boil, stirring all the time. Check seasoning. Pour over the chops. Serve with apple sauce.

Charcuterie

It is a pity that the island's charcuteries have disappeared. My husband's uncle, Antoine Houédard, ran a typical one between the wars in the Pollet in St Peter Port with his specialities made on the premises. Pommier's was a similar establishment in Fountain Street where I can remember admiring the beautiful decorated tiling. Now we have to cross to France to find a charcuterie in which to gaze on the multitude of different sausages, pâtés and terrines and to inhale the rich appetising smell. Most of the charcuterie on sale locally is now factory-made and imported.

However, it is easy to make delicious charcuterie in your own home and the quality will be assured because you will have chosen the ingredients yourself, so no worries about those dreaded E numbers and other additives generally lurking in the bought product. Here are three easy recipes.

Pork Terrine

Terrines are coarser than pâtés.

The following quantities are enough for at least ten servings
500g/1lb belly of pork
500g/1lb lean veal (alternatively use lean pork)
250g/8oz pigs liver   Nutmeg
250g/8oz bacon   1 tbsp chopped thyme
90g/3oz white breadcrumbs   1 tbsp chopped majoram
2 cloves garlic   4 or 5 bay leaves
1 tsp juniper berries   2 tbsp brandy or calvados
2 tsp green brined peppercorns   Salt and pepper

Remove any fibrous bits from the liver and roughly chop along with the pork, veal and bacon. Whizz briefly in the food processor or mince roughly (it mustn't be too smooth). Crush the juniper berries in the pestle and mortar or with a rolling pin. Add to the meat along with the chopped cloves of garlic, a good grating of nutmeg, breadcrumbs, green peppercorns, brandy or calvados, salt and pepper and chopped herbs. Allow to rest for about two hours.

Fill a buttered ovenproof terrine pressing the meat down. Lay the bay leaves along the top. Either cover with a lid or greaseproof paper and foil, tying it firmly.

Place in a roasting tin, half filled with water. Cook in a moderate oven for two and a half hours. When cooked, lift from the tin. Remove the bay leaves and using a fork mash the meat so that the fat becomes integrated. Replace the bay leaves or use fresh ones, cover with a piece of greaseproof paper and a board or something rigid that fits the dish. Place weights on top and leave until thoroughly cold. Remove the weights and refrigerate.

Pork Pâté

Serves 6

500g/1lb pigs liver
500g/1lb piece bacon
500g/1lb belly of pork
120g/4oz rashers of streaky bacon
1 plump clove garlic

3 shallots
About 8 crushed juniper berries
1 meagre tsp allspice
Salt and pepper
2 tbsp brandy

Cut the piece of bacon and pork into fairly small pieces and remove any fibrous pipes from the liver. Chop the shallots and garlic. Mix with the meat, place in the food processor and whizz until fairly smooth. Tip into a bowl and add the remaining ingredients and leave to marinate for about two hours. Line a deep terrine with the streaky bacon and spoon in the mixture. Cover with a lid or greaseproof paper and foil. Place in a roasting pan of water and cook slowly in a moderate oven for three hours. Allow to cool, then refrigerate. Turn out and cut into slices and serve with thick apple sauce.

M
E
A
T

Brawn

Brawns are chopped meat set in jelly. Traditionally the head would be used but I wasn't brave enough so opted for the lower leg. Other cuts could include the hand (foreleg or shoulder) or trotters including the knuckle. It is most important to have bones to produce the gelatine in which the meat sets.

Serves 4
1 lower leg of pork weighing approximately 1kilo/2lbs.
1 onion
A good handful of herbs including sage, parsley, bay leaves and thyme
1 tsp each of cloves and juniper berries
A piece of cinnamon stick
4-5 cardamom pods
Salt and pepper
1 lemon
1 tbsp chopped parsley

Place the leg in a large pan. Add the roughly chopped herbs and onion, the broken up cinnamon stick, crushed spices (use the back of a wooden spoon) and lemon juice. Cover with water. Add one tsp salt and a good grinding of black pepper. Bring slowly to the boil and after five minutes, remove the scum from the surface. Simmer gently for at least four hours, topping up with water if necessary.

When cooked, remove the meat. Strain the liquor through a fine sieve, return to the pan and reduce until you have about 275ml/ 10fl oz.

When cool, pick the meat from the bone, discarding some of the fat.

Chop the meat, including some of the skin (use as much as you think you will like). Add the chopped parsley. Spoon into a dish or terrine then pour over the stock and leave to set.

~

Rabbit

Jersey French	wild: *côni* (m), *cinil* (m), *lapin* (m), *sauvage*
	tame: *lapin* (m), *privé*
Guernsey French	*lapin* (m), *lapaenne* (f)

M
E
A
T

Rabbit was an important source of food for both rich and poor. This was one food that the needy could have even if they didn't own a gun. They could catch them by watching their runs and laying snares or by netting as ferrets chased them out. Many of the Seigneurs and bigger farmers had warrens surrounded by deep ditches or a moat to keep the rabbits from escaping. Here, rabbits were bred to eat – no doubt many of those found their way onto a needy man's table.

During the Occupation, rabbits were again bred for food and it was one animal that owners could protect from theft as sheds containing hutches could be locked or, if necessary, brought indoors. Nan du Feu tells me that in Jersey she actually saw a German soldier walking out of the farmyard with a sackful of her rabbits slung over his shoulder. She also mentions that looking for 'rabbit food' from the fields and hedges was like looking for treasure!

Once caught, a rabbit should be emptied, hung outside for two or three days then skinned. Recently a friend offered me a rabbit. It was hanging on the washing-line in its fur coat! I accepted his offer wondering what I had let myself in for but he reassured me by telling me to collect it the next morning. To my relief it was skinned. He must have seen my face because he added, "quite easy, just like peeling a banana."

Young rabbit, whether wild or domesticated, has white flesh. This can often pass as chicken. The older the rabbit gets, the darker the flesh becomes.

M
E
A
T

Rabbit Casserole

Serves 4
1 rabbit
440 ml/15fl oz dry cider (1 can)
1 onion
2 tbsp tomato paste
1 tbsp flour
6 sprigs thyme
2 good sprig rosemary
Flour for coating
Oil for frying
120g/4oz piece of bacon or streaky rashers
1 stick celery
1 carrot
Salt and pepper

If using a wild rabbit, my friend suggested that it should be steeped in brine for several hours to reduce the gamey/wild taste.

Cut the rabbit into portions, front and hind legs and body. To make the stock, place the body in a saucepan with half the herbs, a chopped carrot and stick of celery. Just cover with water and simmer for an hour. Meanwhile, coat the leg pieces in flour and fry until golden. Place in an ovenproof casserole. Fry the sliced onion until soft, scatter over the rabbit. Next fry the chopped bacon, adding it as well. In the pan, sprinkle the flour adding the cider, a little at a time, then the tomato paste. Stirring all the time, bring slowly to the boil. Season and pour over the rabbit. Add the herbs and enough stock to cover the joints. Cover and cook in a moderate oven for about two hours.

Dumplings go well with this dish.

Rabbit Pie

Serves 4
1 rabbit
120g/4oz piece of bacon or rashers
1 onion
2 medium carrots
120g/4oz button mushrooms
1 cooking apple
1 tsp allspice
60g/2oz flour
Oil
Salt and pepper

Pastry
180g/6oz plain flour
60g/2oz lard
60g/2oz butter
2 tbsp water

Cut the rabbit into pieces. Use the body to make stock, as in the previous recipe.

Use some of the flour to coat the pieces and fry in oil until golden. Place in a roomy pie dish that will take a pastry lid.

Fry the sliced onion, followed by the bacon and mushrooms. Scatter over the fried rabbit pieces along with the chopped carrots and peeled and chopped apple. Sprinkle the remaining flour and allspice into the pan, add about 300ml/10fl oz stock and stir until smooth and bubbling. Pour over the rabbit pieces in the pie dish.

Make the pastry in the food processor by rubbing or grating in the fats. Add about two tbsp of cold water and mix to a stiff paste. Roll out, lining the rim of the pie dish then covering it with the rest of the pastry. Brush with beaten egg or milk and cook at 180°C, 350°F, Gas 4 for at least two hours. Cover the pastry with foil when it is golden brown.

~

M
E
A
T

M
E
A
T

Pigeon

| Jersey French | *pigeon* (m) |
| Guernsey French | *pigeaon* (m), *pigeaonne* (f) |

One of the many privileges enjoyed by the Seigneurs was owning a dovecot or *colombier* on their estate or *fief*. These *colombiers* were often beautifully built and housed as many as a thousand pairs of pigeons. They alone could own pigeons which were the bane of the farmer's life who was trying to grow crops. In the Spring they would nip off the heads of young plants. During the summer they would eat or damage fruit, then fatten themselves on the corn left from harvesting so that by October/November there were some very plump pigeons.

M
E
A
T

Pigeon/Poussin Braised with Cabbage

Serves 4

4 ready dressed pigeons or baby chickens/poussin
8 slices of smoked bacon
2 carrots
2 sticks celery
1 onion
1 savoy cabbage
6 juniper berries
60g/2oz butter

Prepare the pigeons/poussins by spreading each with butter then laying two slices of bacon over.

Cut the thick ribs from the cabbage and shred it. Place in a roomy ovenproof casserole. Add the diced carrot, sliced onion, sliced celery and juniper berries. Nestle the pigeons/poussins in amongst the vegetables. Season with salt and pepper. Pour over the cider.

Cover and roast at 230°C, 450° F, Gas 8 for thirty minutes then reducing the heat to a moderate oven for a further forty minutes, removing the lid for the last fifteen minutes.

Remember when serving that finger bowls would be a good idea as they are impossible to eat without using fingers.

The 'Famous 12th' is an August event, i.e. late summer, but most of us don't think about game until the Autumn months. In the islands, the only game now regularly shot is rabbit. Buy some if you can – it is delicious, organic and seasonal! Imported pheasant, grouse, etc., also become available locally in the autumn. As with all game, care must be taken to remove any remaining pellets in the flesh!

M
E
A
T

Pheasant

| Jersey French | *faîsan* (m) |
| Guernsey French | *faisànt* (m) |

Braised Pheasant with Red Cabbage

Serves 6

2 dressed pheasants
Half red cabbage
1 tbsp Demerara sugar
1 level tsp ground cloves
1 tbsp wine vinegar
2 onions
1 bramley apple

6 juniper berries
440 ml/15fl oz/1 can dry cider
Salt and black pepper
2-3 bay leaves
180g/6oz bacon
Flour for coating & 1 tbsp for sauce
Oil for frying

Wash the pheasants then cut each into four portions. The portions may be left on the bone but I choose to remove much of the bone and the leg sinews as this makes eating so much more enjoyable. Boning doesn't take long and even if the leg looks a mess, once floured, fried and embedded in the red cabbage, it looks quite respectable.

Coat the pieces in flour and fry until golden, followed by the sliced onion and bacon. While this takes place, slice the cabbage, removing the centre and fibrous ribs. Peel and chop the apples. Scatter the cabbage and apple in a roomy casserole, sprinkle with the sugar, ground cloves and vinegar, turning the lot to mix well. Place the fried pieces of pheasant on top, followed by the fried chopped onion and bacon. In the pan, scatter one tbsp flour, add the cider and seasoning, stir well and bring slowly to the boil. Add the crushed juniper berries and pour over the pheasant. Place the bay leaves on top.

Cover and cook in a moderate oven for about two hours. Check to make sure that it hasn't dried out adding more water or cider if necessary.

Serve with boiled or mashed potatoes.

~

F
I
S
H

Sea Bream

| Jersey French | *brême* (f), *sarde* (f) |
| Guernsey French | *sarde naër* (f), *brême* (f) |

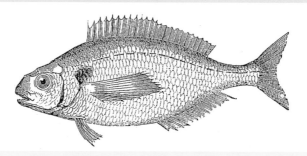

Baked Black Sea Bream with a Four Herb Sauce

Serves 4
4 Black Bream weighing approx 500g/1lb each
1 lemon
Salt and pepper

Sauce

1 tbsp chopped parsley
1 tbsp chopped mint
1 tbsp chopped coriander
1 tbsp scissored chives
4 anchovy fillets

1 clove garlic
1 tsp Dijon mustard
1 tbsp olive oil
Salt and pepper
4 wedges of lemon

Scale, gut and carefully wash the bream. Start by removing the spiny fins running along the top and underside of the bream. Use scissors or a sharp knife to remove them but take care as they are particularly nasty.

Make three vertical slashes on each side and lay in a roasting pan, or if you prefer, the bream can just as easily be grilled. Squeeze the lemon and pour the juice into the slashes. Season. Turn the fish and repeat.

Place the bream in a hot oven for about twenty minutes or under the grill for about five minutes each side.

As the fish cooks, make the sauce.

In the food processor place the coriander, parsley and mint, the scissored chives and the flattened (use the blade of a knife) clove of garlic. Roughly chop and add the anchovy fillets and finally the mustard and pepper. Whizz, slowly adding the olive oil until fairly smooth.

Serve the sauce separately or spoon over the fish with extra wedges of lemon.

F
I
S
H

~

Pollack/Whiting

| Jersey French | *lieu* (m) |
| Guernsey French | *lu* (m) hp, *liotin* (m) lp |

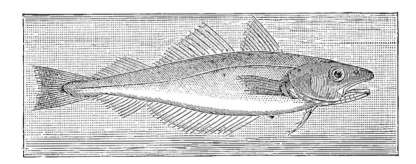

This is one of my favourite local fish. Just floured and fried in butter and served with a wedge of lemon it is delicious.

It can be steamed in the oven with white wine and a few herbs. The cooking juice can be used to make a white sauce with lots of chopped parsley and chives so that it is really green and quite runny. Then all that is needed is lots of mopping up material!

F
I
S
H

Baked Skate with Caper Sauce

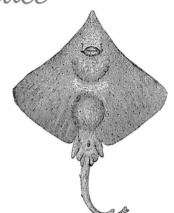

Serves 4
4 pieces of skate wing,
  each weighing about 250g/8oz
1 lemon
3 tbsp capers
2 tbsp chopped parsley
1 tbsp chopped sage
1 tbsp chopped chives
150ml/5fl oz double cream

Olive oil for brushing the skate wings

Brush the wings with oil. Lay them in an oiled and roomy roasting pan with two tbsp water to prevent them sticking. Roast at 215°C, 425°F, Gas 7 for approximately fifteen minutes until well cooked. Remove the wings from the pan, cover and keep warm.

In the pan add the lemon juice, herbs and capers. When bubbling, stir in the cream. Pour over the wings. Serve with finely shredded cooked cabbage tossed in butter.

~

Autumn is a time for a change in vegetables; carrots are becoming more mature while other roots are just beginning to appear. Leeks are making a welcome return and those lucky enough to have horses grazing in their fields may find mushrooms. The quality of cabbages and cauliflowers seems better during the cooler months. Tomatoes continue but that delicious flavour of the summer months is fading. Herbs continue to be good.

Beetroot

| Jersey French | *betterave* (f) |
| Guernsey French | *rouge baette* (f), *bétrave* (f) |

Beetroot tends to be used as a salad vegetable but is very good eaten hot or made into a soup.

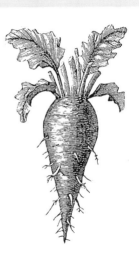

Take approximately 500g/1lb of cooked beetroot. Cut it into strips and in a pan, toss in butter and the juice of half a lemon. Add one tbsp chopped parsley, a pinch of sugar and one tbsp chopped capers.

Another way is to toss the beetroot strips in a pan with one tbsp cider vinegar, one tbsp runny honey, salt and pepper and when bubbling, add two tbsp double cream or crème fraîche.

~

Carrots

Jersey French	*cârotte* (f)
Guernsey French	*cârotte* (f)

Main crop carrots are usually harvested around mid-October. This is another versatile vegetable which can be used in many different ways. They add colour to any dish.

In the past, they were used a lot in cooking as a sweetner. I can remember carrots grown for the farm, they were the size of parsnips – dark orange and very sweet. Not only did my horse enjoy them but the family too!

To make carrots more interesting, peel and cut them into strips. Gently fry two or three finely sliced shallots in butter, or one small sliced onion. Add the carrot strips, mix until well coated. Sprinkle with a pinch of sugar and a little water. Cover and cook for about ten minutes. On serving, scatter with finely chopped parsley.

Carrot & Ginger Soup

Serves 4

500g/1lb carrots	1 tbsp finely grated fresh ginger
30g/1oz butter	1 tsp curry powder or curry paste
1 medium onion	800ml/1.5 pints vegetable or chicken stock
1 potato	Salt and pepper
1 clove garlic	

To serve

4 tbsp double cream
Juice of half a lemon
1 tbsp chopped parsley

Cook the chopped onion and garlic in the butter until soft. Add the chopped carrots and potato.

Stir in the grated ginger and curry powder or curry paste.

Add the stock. Season. Cover and simmer for thirty to forty minutes.

Cool, then liquidize the soup until smooth. Return to the pan. Check seasoning.

When ready to serve, heat the soup adding the lemon juice. When hot, stir in the cream and chopped parsley. Serve either individually or in a soup tureen. Alternatively, swirl the cream over the soup in the tureen to give a ripple effect and scatter with parsley.

Carrot & Coriander Soup

Serves 4
Use the same ingredients as above, replacing the curry powder or paste and ginger with a good handful of torn, fresh coriander.

Carrot & Tarragon Salad

Grated carrots scattered with fresh tarragon leaves, finely sliced spring onion and dressed with a vinaigrette made with lemon juice rather than vinegar goes well with roasted cold meats, especially chicken and with baked cold fish.

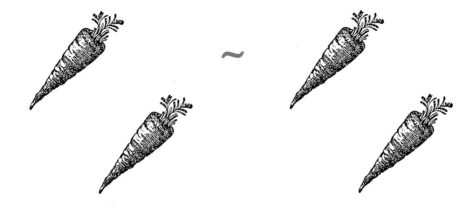

V
E
G
E
T
A
B
L
E
S

Cauliflower

Jersey French   *chou-fleur* (m), *brécolin* (m), *brécoli* (m)
Guernsey French   *chouflleur* (m), *broccôlu* (m)

Cauliflower was a vegetable that came into season in the autumn and carried on throughout the winter but now it is available all year round. I still like to think of it as an autumn and winter vegetable.

Cauliflower & Potato Pie

Serves 4
500g/1lb cauliflower florets
500g/1lb potatoes
3 tbsp double cream
Grated nutmeg

60g/2oz hard cheese, grated
Salt and pepper
30g/1oz flour
30g/1oz butter
150ml/5fl oz full cream milk

Cube the potato into pieces about the same size as the florets. Boil both together in salted water for ten minutes. Drain and put into an ovenproof casserole. Reserve some of the vegetable water.
Melt the butter in a small pan, add the flour and grated nutmeg. Mix. Gradually add the milk and cream until you have a thick, smooth consistency. Add a little of the vegetable water if necessary. Season. Pour over the vegetables, scatter with cheese and bake in the oven or under the grill.

Cauliflower Cream Soup

Serves 4
1 medium sized cauliflower
800ml/30fl oz chicken stock
150ml/5fl oz double cream
30g/1oz butter
30g/1oz ground almonds
1 tbsp toasted flaked almonds

1 onion
A good handful of sprigs of
    lemon or ordinary thyme
1 tbsp chopped chives
Salt and pepper

In a roomy pan, fry the chopped onion in the butter. Add the cauliflower florets, thyme, ground almonds and chicken stock. Season. Simmer for thirty minutes. Strain and sieve or mouli, returning to the pan, then bring to the boil. Away from the heat, stir in the cream, scattering the chives and flaked almonds on top.

~

Onions

Jersey French	ouognon (m)
Guernsey French	ougniaon (m)

Onions can be harvested from late summer into autumn. It is a huge family, there are brown, golden, purple and white ones. Some are tall and skinny while others are short and squat; there are also the clusters of shallots. No matter the size, shape or colour, onions must be one of our most popular vegetables.

An onion that has been allowed to mature slowly until the tops are brown and dry, then baked whole in its skin is something worth waiting for all year. In fact, any onion cooked this way is always a winner.

Bread, cheese and onion have been a staple meal for many a worker. Fried onions go with almost everything; their tempting smell is enough to get the saliva glands going. Onion skins also have their use. The papery skins if added to a broth or soup will add a natural golden colour and they are still used for dying wool a soft amber colour.

Onions with Gammon

Serves 4
4 large or 8 medium onions
A piece of gammon or bacon weighing
  about 18og/6oz
Bay leaves
Salt and pepper

V
E
G
E
T
A
B
L
E
S

Put the peeled onions in a casserole big enough to hold them snugly.

Chop the gammon or bacon, scattering it over the onions making sure some goes to the bottom. Add two tblsp of water, seasoning and two or three bay leaves. Cover with a tightly fitting lid or foil and cook at 200°C, 400°F, Gas 6 for one hour.

Onion Soup

Serves 4
750g/1.5 lbs onions
4 rounds of bread per person, if possible French bread
4 tbsp grated cheese
2 or 3 leaves of torn sage leaves
3 sprigs of thyme
800ml/1.5pints of chicken or vegetable stock
60g/2oz butter
30g/1oz flour
Good pinch of sugar
Salt and pepper
150 ml/5fl oz dry cider

In a roomy saucepan, fry the thinly sliced onions in the butter until soft and golden. Add the flour, sugar, seasoning, herbs, cider and stock. Allow to simmer for at least one hour. Just before serving, pile the cheese on the rounds of bread and grill until the cheese is golden and bubbling. Either pour the soup into a tureen or into individual bowls. Using a fish slice float the cheesy bread in the tureen or bowls.

~

Mushrooms

| Jersey French | *champîngnon* (m) |
| Guernsey French | *chàmpignaön* (m) |

V
E
G
E
T
A
B
L
E
S

Seeing how many mushrooms we could find in the neighbouring fields was a game we children used to play – alas, modern farming methods are probably to blame for the virtual disappearance of the simple wild mushroom locally, although other forms of edible wild fungus are still around. Specialist knowledge is needed before any wild fungus is picked to be eaten – they can be extremely poisonous. Years ago, my sister-in-law gave me a puffball, telling me it was perfectly safe to eat. She suggested slicing it and frying it in butter which I did – I survived, but have no particular inclination to repeat the experiment!

Mushrooms with Bacon

Serves 2
250g/8oz mushrooms
6 rashers of smoked streaky bacon
30g/1oz butter
2 eggs
60g/2oz cheese, grated
150ml/5fl oz double cream
Small bunch of chives
Salt and pepper

Cut the bacon into strips and fry in the butter. Remove from the pan and in the same buttery juices, fry the sliced mushroom very briefly as prolonged cooking makes them shrink. Share the bacon and mushrooms between two small ovenproof dishes. Beat the eggs. Add the cream, seasoning and scissor in the chives. Pour over the bacon and mushrooms. Sprinkle with cheese and bake at 180°C, 350°F, Gas 4 until set, about thirty minutes.

VEGETABLES

Stuffed Mushrooms

Serves 4
8 flat mushrooms
4 tbsp white breadcrumbs
2 tbsp chopped parsley
1 tsp chopped tarragon leaves
1 very finely chopped onion
Grated rind of 1 lemon
1 egg
30g/1oz chopped walnuts
90g/3oz hard cheese
2 tbsp double cream
Salt and pepper

Place the mushrooms, stalk side up, on a baking sheet. In a bowl, beat the egg. Add the remaining ingredients. Share between the mushrooms. Scatter with the grated cheese. Bake at 180°C, 350°F, Gas 4 for thirty minutes. Serve on rounds of fried bread or toast with twisted finely cut slices of the lemon.

~

Jerusalem Artichoke

Jersey French   *paithe* (f) *dé tèrre*

This vegetable is thought to have been brought to Europe from North America early in the seventeenth century. It has a distinctive flavour, faintly reminiscent of the globe artichoke. The name has nothing to do with the city of Jerusalem. It is a member of the sunflower family and its English name probably stems from the Italian word for sunflower which is *girasole*.

Eaten cold, after boiling, they make a delicious salad, dressed liberally with a vinaigrette and sprinkled with chopped parsley and/or chives. They also make a distinctive soup or pie.

Jerusalem Artichoke Pie

Serves 6
500g/1lb artichokes (about 250g/
  8oz trimmed weight)
30g/1oz butter
3 egg yolks
1 tbsp finely chopped hazelnuts
2 tbsp grated parmesan

1 tbsp chopped parsley
Salt and pepper
Pastry case
180g/6oz plain flour
120g/4oz butter

Start by making the pastry case and lining a 23 cm/9 inch pie or flan dish. Prick the base, line with foil making sure it comes up and over the top to prevent the sides falling in. Chill for thirty minutes. Bake for twenty minutes at 200°C, 400°F, Gas 6.

Peel the artichokes and boil until tender about ten to fifteen minutes. Pass through a sieve into a bowl. Add melted butter, beaten egg yolks, hazelnuts, parsley and parmesan. Season and pour into the baked pastry case. Cook for twenty minutes at 180°C, 350°F, Gas 4 until set. Cool a little and serve in wedges with a watercress and rocket salad.

V
E
G
E
T
A
B
L
E
S

Jerusalem Artichokes with Scallops

Serves 4

12 scallops
375g/12oz Jerusalem Artichokes
60g/2oz butter
120ml/4fl oz white wine

1 tbsp chopped parsley
2 tbsp lemon juice
2 tbsp double cream
Salt and pepper

Peel, slice and cut the artichokes into fingers. Cook in a pan in the butter until tender, about ten to fifteen minutes. Remove, cover and keep warm. Slice the scallops in half and fry in the butter, about two minutes each side. Remove and keep them warm. Add the wine and lemon juice to the pan, simmer until reduced a little, then stir in the parsley and cream. Season.

To serve scatter the artichokes over the scallops and pour over the hot sauce.

~

Cabbage

| Jersey French | caboche (m) |
| Guernsey French | caboche (f) |

This is a much maligned vegetable and the butt of many a joke about lodgings at seaside resorts such as Blackpool! My childhood memories are likewise coloured by the all-pervading smell, probably resulting from overcooking.

Of course, cabbage can be delicious eaten raw, in salads and slaws – this clearly overcomes the smell problem. Stir frying is another method to minimise the smell. The cabbage family is large, ranging from creamy white to dark green and, of course, red. There are loose-leaved cabbages and tightly-packed, wrinkly or smooth ones. The giant Jersey cabbage is mentioned on page 42.

Cabbage Soup

This is a favourite local recipe that has been handed down through generations.

Serves 4

1 medium cabbage	1 litre/2 pints vegetable or chicken stock
3 onions	2/3 sprigs thyme
2 carrots	2 bay leaves
2 leeks	Salt and pepper
2 potatoes	30g/1oz butter

In a saucepan, fry the sliced onion and leek. Add the diced carrot and potato, the stock, seasoning, thyme and bay leaves. Simmer for thirty minutes. Remove and discard the main rib from the cabbage leaves. Stack and finely slice the leaves, adding them to the soup. Simmer for twenty minutes. Check seasoning and serve.

A good cupful of peas is often added.

The Gwendoline Roberts Cabbage Soup

I have prepared the following more robust cabbage soup recipe from information provided by La Société Guernesiase – unfortunately, Gwendoline forgot to specify quantities for the ingredients so I have had to 'guestimate' these!

1 medium smooth leaved cabbage	1 kilo/ 21bs brisket of beef
6 celery sticks	500g /1lb potatoes
2 medium onions	60g/2oz rice (half breakfast cup)
Mixed herbs	Seasoning

Braise the beef in plenty of water with the chopped celery, onions and herbs added. Then, when the meat is cooked, slice and add the cabbage and potatoes along with the rice. Season to taste.

Traditionally the clear soup from this concoction was served as the first course accompanied by snippets of bread. The meat and vegetables were then served, in the same plates as the second course. This certainly saves on the washing up!

Gwendoline explains that on weekdays the soup spoons were silver but the forks were three-pronged steel affairs with boxwood handles. The description of the forks suggests early Victorian times. On Sundays and holidays all the cutlery would be silver. I think most farm people lived this way and much of the silver would boast Guernsey silversmiths' marks.

The pudding that followed would surely have been roly-poly or just possibly fruit or bread and cheese.

Gwendoline adds that on Sunday there would be a huge joint of beef cooked in *le vier four*, together with the best rice pudding ever tasted, large baked apples or, in winter, a croc of pears cooked with white sugar, cloves and red wine.

Cabbage Salad

Cabbage comes in very useful as a salad vegetable and the white one is the best to use. Many additions can be made such as grated carrot, beetroot, onion and many herbs. A variety of vinaigrettes or mayonnaise may be used to dress it.

Serves 4

500g/ 8oz finely shredded
   white cabbage
2 carrots
1 dessert apple
3 spring onions
3 tbsp cider vinegar   1 tsp sugar
125ml/5fl oz mayonnaise   1 tsp celery seed
125ml/5fl oz soured cream   Tabasco
   or crème fraîche   Salt and pepper

Place the cabbage in a roomy bowl. Add the grated carrot, apple and finely sliced spring onion. In a small bowl, mix the remaining ingredients. Add to the cabbage and turn until all is well coated. Chill before serving.

Leeks

| Jersey French | pouothé (m) |
| Guernsey French | pouorraïe (f) |

V
E
G
E
T
A
B
L
E
S

Leek Timbales

Serves 4

3 leeks	150 ml/5fl oz double cream
2 eggs	1 tbsp chopped parsley
3 tbsp white breadcrumbs	A grating of nutmeg
2 rashers of smoked streaky bacon	Salt and pepper

Trim and slice the leeks almost to the base. Wash carefully, then cook in boiling, salted water for five minutes. When cool enough to handle, take the outer leaves and line four well buttered timbales or breakfast cups ensuring that they overlap. Fry the finely chopped bacon. In the food processor whizz the roughly chopped remainder of the leek. Add the eggs, cream, parsley, nutmeg, breadcrumbs and seasoning. Whizz again. Spoon into the timbales. Sprinkle over the bacon then fold the leek over the top and cover with tin-foil. Place in a roasting tin with water half way up. Cook for forty minutes at 180°C, 350°F, Gas 4. Remove from the tin, relax them for fifteen minutes, run a knife around the edge and turn out.

Baked Leeks with Cheese

Serves 4

4 to 6 leeks depending on size	Salt and pepper
120g/4oz Cheddar cheese, grated	Grated nutmeg
4 tbsp double cream	Butter for greasing the dish
60g/2oz hazelnuts	

Toast the hazelnuts then rub off as much of the skin as possible and finely chop them. Carefully wash the leeks, cutting them in half down the middle. Boil in salted water for five minutes. Drain them. Butter the ovenproof dish and sprinkle half the cheese in the bottom. Arrange the leeks on top. Scatter with the chopped hazelnuts and remaining cheese. Pour over the cream. Season with salt, pepper and a grating of nutmeg. Bake in a hot oven for twenty minutes.

V
E
G
E
T
A
B
L
E
S

Pumpkin

Jersey French	*pompon* (m), *potithon* (m)
Guernsey French	*paömpaön* (m)

Pumpkins appear in October and have now become part of the Halloween celebrations when they are carved into mainly ghoulish faces and emptied to hold candles. The original pumpkin is round with a ribbed appearance, orange in colour and can keep for up to six months. It tastes bland so needs other ingredients to make it more interesting.

Pumpkin Soup

Serves 4
750g/1.5lbs pumpkin
1 onion
1 leek
500g/1lb skinned tomatoes
Half tsp ground cummin
Half tsp ground coriander
30g/1oz butter
800ml/1.5pts chicken stock or water
3 tbsp cream
2 tsp scissored chives
3 rashers of crisply fried bacon (optional)
Salt and pepper

Soften the chopped onion in butter, add the sliced leek and cook until soft. Add the pumpkin in smallish chunks, the chopped up tomatoes, ground cumin, coriander and seasoning. Add the stock or water and simmer for thirty to forty minutes. Whizz in the blender.

Serve in bowls or a soup tureen, swirling the cream on top and scatter with scissored chives. The addition of the crisply fried bacon at the last minute gives added interest.

Pumpkin Salad

Serves 4
500g/8oz peeled pumpkin
6-8 coriander leaves
1 tbsp black mustard seeds
3 tbsp sunflower oil
1 tbsp soy sauce
2 tbsp lemon juice
1 tbspsoft brown sugar
1 level tsp ground cummin
Salt and pepper

In a roomy bowl, combine the grated pumpkin, torn coriander leaves and mustard seeds. In a small bowl make the dressing by mixing the oil, soy sauce, lemon juice, sugar, salt and pepper. Pour half over the pumpkin, turning everything then refrigerate for thirty minutes. Just before serving, add the remaining dressing.

~

Celery

Jersey French	*celeri* (m)
Guernsey French	*celeri* (m)

Celery is mainly used as a salad vegetable but is equally tasty when cooked. The tough outer stems make excellent soups while the more tender inner ones can be used in salads or eaten on their own with cheese.

V
E
G
E
T
A
B
L
E
S

Cream of Celery Soup

Serves 4

I head of celery weighing 300g/10oz
30g/1oz butter
30g/1oz flour
A handful of parsley: about 30g/1oz
150ml/5fl oz double cream
2 tbsp scissored chives

1 onion
800ml/1.5pints chicken
   or vegetable stock
Salt and pepper
Grated nutmeg

Roughly chop the cleaned celery and onion. Gently fry in the butter in a roomy pan. Stir in the flour and seasoning. Add the stock and roughly chopped parsley. Simmer for about thirty minutes until the celery is cooked. Pass through a sieve or mouli. Reheat, and on reaching boiling point, remove from the heat, stir in the cream and chives. Pour into soup bowls with a little grated nutmeg on top. Serve with croûtons.

Braised Celery with Ham

Serves 4
2 medium heads of celery
4 slices cooked ham
30g/1oz butter

Sauce
30g/1oz butter
30g/1oz flour
275ml/10fl oz milk

Salt and pepper
Grated nutmeg
60g/2oz cheddar cheese

Remove any tough outer leaves, wash the head and cut vertically in half. Place in a pan with a little salt. Cover with water, bring to the boil and cook for ten minutes.
Drain but keep the water. Wrap the heads in slices of ham and place them in an oblong ovenproof dish.
Make the sauce by melting the butter and stirring in the flour. Gradually add the milk and a little of the cooking water if necessary. Season. When creamy and bubbling, pour over the celery. Scatter the cheese on top. Sprinkle a little grated nutmeg.
Bake in a medium oven until bubbling and golden.

Apples

| Jersey French | pomme (f) |
| Guernsey French | paomme (f) |

The apple must surely be the best known and popular of fruits. Involved in the downfall of Adam and Eve and later inspiring Newton in his Theory of Gravity, in today's health-concious society most of us now concur with the 'An apple a day' adage. If ever there was a healthy, convenience 'fast food' then it must be the apple!

Every cook knows very well how to use apples in a variety of ways so, apart from daring to mention apple pie and baked apples, I will include only one other recipe here. (See page 59 for Apple Pudding; page 60 for Apple Cake).

Celery & Apple Soup

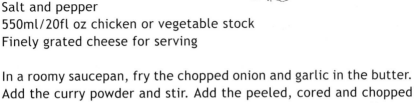

Serves 4
1 large onion
60g/2oz butter
1 fat clove garlic
1 large Bramley apple
1 eating apple
4-6 stalks celery (depending on size)
1 dessertspoon medium curry powder
Half lemon
Salt and pepper
550ml/20fl oz chicken or vegetable stock
Finely grated cheese for serving

In a roomy saucepan, fry the chopped onion and garlic in the butter. Add the curry powder and stir. Add the peeled, cored and chopped apples and chopped celery. Cover with the stock and squeezed lemon juice. Season. Cover and simmer for about forty-five minutes. Cool a little and then sieve or use the blender. Check seasoning.

Serve hot with a bowl of finely grated cheese and croûtons.

F
R
U
I
T

Apple Pie

Jersey French	*du Solyi*
Guernsey French	*d'la Gâche à Paommes*

Like gâche mêlaïe, apple pie is a longstanding favourite. Thinly sliced apples with a few cloves and a sprinkling of sugar, sandwiched between two layers of pastry and baked to perfection, have been a winning combination from time immemorial. Also like gâche mêlaïe, apple pie is good hot or cold.

Honey Glazed Cinnamon Baked Apples

Core cooking apples but don't peel them. Stuff the centre with dried fruit such as currants, sultanas or raisins. Add a dusting of ground cinnamon or ginger, a drizzle of honey and a little water to prevent them sticking. Baked slowly in a moderate oven until they split and begin to collapse and served with double cream, the result is truly delicious.

~

Quince

Jersey French	*coing* (m)

Don't be misled – its sour, dry flesh is most unappetising when raw. However, cooked and sweetened, the quince possesses a most attractive flavour, as well as colour. Apple pie becomes extra special with the addition of some quince which can also be made into a delicious coral-coloured jelly.

Upside down Apple & Quince Tart with Bramble Sauce

Serves 4
500g/1lb cooking apples
250g/half lb quince
90g/3oz sugar
6 cloves

Pastry
120g/4oz flour
90g/3oz butter plus a little extra
    for greasing the baking tin or dish

Sauce
500g/1lb blackberries
120g/4oz sugar
2 tsp arrowroot or cornflour
150ml/5fl oz water

Make the pastry by grating the butter into the flour. Add a little water to mix to a stiff paste. Peel and slice the apple and quince finely. Pile into a well greased dish. Add the sugar and cloves. Cover with the lid of pastry so that it is well tucked in and the fruit well sealed. Bake in a moderate oven for forty-five minutes. Allow to cool a little.

Make the sauce by stewing the blackberries in the water for ten minutes.

Push through a fine sieve into a pan. Dissolve the cornflour or arrowroot in a little water. Add it with the sugar to the blackberry juice. Slowly bring to the boil. Boil for two minutes adding a little water if too thick.

To serve, run a knife around the dish. Invert the upside-down tart onto a plate and serve with the sauce.

F
R
U
I
T

Pear

| Jersey French | *paithe* (f) |
| Guernsey French | *père* (f) |

The pears most widely grown in the Islands are probably Conference, William's (also known as the Bartlett) and Doyenne du Comice. In the past, the favourites appear to have been Louise Bonne of Jersey, Chaumontel and Duchesse d'Angoulême. A document dated 1616 in the States of Guernsey Archives refers to *poires sidrées*, suggesting that perry was made at the time, though the variety of pear employed is not known.

Pears poached in Cider with Chocolate sauce

Serves 4

4 dessert pears
1 lemon
90g/3oz sugar
1 can/440ml cider
   or Rocquette cider
Powdered cinnamon

Sauce
120g/4oz dark chocolate
2 tsp powdered coffee or 3 tbsp
   strong black coffee
60g/2oz sugar
150ml/5fl oz single cream

Pare the lemon. Heat the pared lemon strips, cider, sugar and lemon juice and simmer for five minutes. Meanwhile, peel and core the pears standing them upright so that they fit tightly in an ovenproof dish. Pour over the cider mixture and dust the pears with cinnamon. Cover and cook at 190°C, 375°F, Gas 5 for thirty minutes. Remove from the oven and let them cool.

In a double boiler or bowl inverted in a pan of simmering water, put the chocolate and coffee (if using powdered coffee, dissolve in a little water). When the chocolate has melted, add the sugar and gradually stir in the cream. When thoroughly mixed and smooth put to one side until needed.

Serve the pears with the chocolate sauce poured over.

Croc of Pears

I came across an old recipe using vine leaves. In an earthenware pot layer small tender vine leaves with peeled and halved pears until nearly full, adding a dusting of ground ginger and a few cloves. The pot is filled to the top with cider, covered and cooked gently in an oven for as long as possible, even overnight.

I have tried this recipe and it is good, especially accompanied with some whipped cream.

Pear & Almond Tart

Serves 6/8
Pastry
180g/6oz flour
120g/4oz butter

Filling
4-5 pears
90g/3oz butter
90g/3oz sugar
90g/3oz ground almonds
2 eggs
1 tsp almond essence

Make the pastry in a food processor or grate or rub the butter into the flour, binding it with a little water. Line a 23 cm/9 inch flan tin.

Peel and core the pears. Finely slice them, radiating them in the pastry case.

Place all the remaining ingredients in the food processor. Whizz until well mixed. Spoon over the pears. Bake at 190°C, 375°F, Gas five for forty-five minutes.

Serve warm or cold with cream.

Pears make a very good salad.

Slice dessert pears, pour over a vinaigrette made with french mustard, lemon juice, olive oil and seasoning. Gently turn so that the pears are well coated. Snip chives on top and sprinkle with toasted chopped walnuts.

Blackberries

F
R
U
I
T

Jersey French	*mouaithe* (f)
Guernsey French	*maëure* (f)

Picking blackberries is an outing to look forward to each year. I can remember my aunt making a special excursion to Herm, a small island off Guernsey, just to pick them. Children love picking them, returning with fingers stained purple, pretending they have been on some gory outing!

During the Occupation of the islands, when food was extremely scarce, blackberries and elderberries replaced dried fruits. Blackberry leaves were also dried and chopped and used as a substitute for tea.

Blackberry Fool

Serves 4
500g/1lb of blackberries

4 tbsp sugar
275ml/10fl oz cream

Cover the blackberries with water. Add the sugar and gently simmer for thirty minutes. Sieve and leave until cold. Whip the cream and fold in the blackberry purée, test for sweetness. Spoon into individual cups or glasses. Chill.

A guide when making fruit fools is to have about equal quantities of thick pureé and cream.

NINTH MONTH **SEPTEMBER** THIRTY DAYS

Blackberry & Apple Crumble

Serves 4
375g/12oz blackberries
2 plump bramley or cooking apples
120g/4oz demerara sugar

Crumble
60g/2oz butter
60g/2oz flour
60g/2oz demerara sugar

In an ovenproof dish, scatter the blackberries, finely sliced apple and sugar.

Make the crumble by grating or rubbing the butter into the flour. Add the sugar and cover the fruit. Dust with ground cinnamon. Bake at 180°C, 350°F, Gas 4 for thirty to forty minutes.

Serve with cream or crème fraîche.

Sloes

Jersey French	*prunelle* (f), *bloche* (f)
Guernsey French	*prunelle* (f)

The pure white starry flowers of the blackthorn are a sign that Spring is in the air. The cliffs and lanes are ablaze with patches of white on somewhat bare branches. In time these flowers turn into little velvety purple bullets, smaller than damsons and as sour or even more so. Often, while picking black-berries, one finds overhead or nearby a blackthorn bush with purple sloes hiding on its spiky branches. Sloes cannot be eaten on their own because of their dry astringent taste. In addition to being the main flavouring in Sloe Gin (an excellent digestif and still popular in the islands), sloes are added when making bramble or apple jelly to enhance the results.

Traditionally, sloes were believed to cure mouth ulcers – having bitten one, taking the cure must have been quite an ordeal!

Before leaving Autumn here are a few recipes for the Store Cupboard:

Chutneys, Pickles, Jellies, Jams & Beverages

In the past, an important autumnal activity was the preserving, in one way or another, of a wide range of fruits and vegetables. I can remember the excitement when my Mother bought a canning machine. The novelty soon wore off as the tightly packed and sealed tins had to be boiled in the copper for a certain time and then plunged into baths of cold water. I'm sure that my Mother soon asked herself if it was worth all that effort to be rewarded in January with some rather limp, discoloured runner beans!

Next came domestic deep freezers, which threatened the demise of those Kilner jars, although certain fruits – peaches, nectarines and cherries, for example – still seem to keep better in Kilner jars, in syrup, than in the deep freeze.

I remember Tante Madeleine telling the sad story of her store of cherries preserved in cognac which disappeared during the Occupation. No doubt whoever found them left behind nothing but the stones.

I have to confess that my own preserving activity is these days limited to making jams, marmalades, jellies and chutneys – my husband describes our bramble jelly as 'winter sunshine'.

Red Tomato Chutney

3 kilos/6lbs red tomatoes	2 bananas
500g/1lb apples	1 tsp cayenne pepper
500g/1lb onions	30g/1oz salt
2 red chillies	2tsp pickling spice
500g/1lb brown sugar	550ml/1pint malt vinegar
250g/8oz raisins	1 tbsp green ginger
1 tbsp curry powder	half tbsp ground cloves

In a roomy pan, put the skinned and chopped tomatoes, peeled and chopped apples and onions and vinegar. Add the salt, sugar, raisins, cayenne pepper, spices, curry powder and chillies. Finally, add the pickling spice in a muslin bag. Simmer gently for one and a half hours then add the sliced bananas and cook until thick. Remove the pickling spice. Pot and seal.

Plum Chutney

3 kilos/6lbs plums
500g/1lb cooking apples
120g/4oz raisins
4 large onions
1.5litres/60fl oz malt vinegar
1kilo 750g/3.5lbs sugar

1 tbsp salt
6 chopped cloves garlic
4 small red chillies
1 tbsp ground allspice
1 tbsp ground ginger
Juice of 1 lemon

Halve the plums removing the stones. Place in a large pan with the peeled and chopped apples and onions. Add the remaining ingredients. Simmer for about two and a half hours until thick. Pot and seal while still hot.

Apple Chutney

30g/1oz ground ginger
15g/half oz garlic
30g/1oz mustard seed
1 tsp cayenne pepper

3 kilos/6lbs cooking apples
1 kilo/2lbs brown sugar
750g/1.5lb onions
1 litre/2pints malt vinegar
750g/1.5lbs sultanas or raisins

Peel and chop the apples. Place in a large pan with the chopped onions, sugar and vinegar. Simmer until soft and pulpy. Add the remaining ingredients and simmer until thick. Pot and seal.

Pickles

| Jersey French | du picl'ye (m) |
| Guernsey French | du picquet (m) |

Spiced vinegar is readily available but it can be made at home.

Place 1litre/2pints of malt vinegar in a bowl. Add 7g/quarter oz each of whole cloves, mace, allspice, white peppercorns and a 6cm/2.5inch piece of cinnamon stick. For a hotter pickle include 7g/quarter oz of crushed chillies and 30g/1oz mustard seed. Put the bowl in a pan of water and bring slowly to the boil, simmering for thirty minutes. Remove from the heat and allow to cool. Once cool, pass through a sieve into a jug.

When pickling, try to use coarse salt as it is purer.

Take care when sealing. A good seal will prevent the vegetables shrinking. Store the jars in a cool place.

Pickled Onions &/or Shallots

3kilos/6lbs of onions or shallots
Coarse salt
1 litre/2pints spiced vinegar

In a large bowl, place the unpeeled onions/shallots in brine. Make the brine by dissolving 120g/4oz salt in a jug with water. Pour over the onions and steep for at least twelve hours.

Drain and peel the onions/shallots and steep again in freshly made brine for a further thirty to thirty-six hours.

Drain and rinse them. Pack tightly into jars, pouring over the spiced vinegar.

Seal and leave for three months before using.

Shallot, Cucumber & Cauliflower Pickle

3kilos/6lbs of a mixture of peeled shallots, peeled and diced cucumber and cauliflower florets.
Place the washed vegetables in a bowl and scatter with 120g/4oz coarse salt. Mix thoroughly and leave for twenty-four hours.
Rinse then pack into jars. Cover with spiced vinegar, pushing a red chilli into each jar. Seal and leave for two months

~

Jellies

Jersey French	*gelée* (f)
Guernsey French	*d'la g'laie* (f)

I find the easiest way to see if jam or jelly is set is the 'saucer' method. When the jam or jelly has boiled for the required time, drop a little on a cold saucer to become quite cold. Then push the jam or jelly with your finger and if it wrinkles, it is ready. If still runny, boil until the wrinkled effect is reached. Pot and seal with waxed paper and tightly fitting lids or jam pot covers.

Mint Jelly

One of Jenny's recipes, a dear friend who now lives in New Zealand

3 kilos/6 lbs cooking apples   Sugar
1 litre 275ml/2.5 pints water   Half litre/1 pint chopped mint

Roughly chop the apples - no peeling or coring necessary. Simmer in the water until a soft pulp. Place a muslin cloth over a wide colander, over a bowl and tip in the pulp. Tie it and hang overnight to drip. Measure the juice and put in a pan. Add 500g/1lb sugar to every 550ml/1pint of juice. Bring slowly to the boil. Add the mint. Boil for about fifteen minutes. Test for setting. Add a few drops of green colouring if you would like a brighter green. Pot in small pots while still hot.

Bramble Jelly

Gather as many blackberries as you think you will need, if possible including a handful of sloes. Place them in a pan and just cover with water. Simmer for about thirty minutes. Follow the same steps as with the mint jelly adding sugar in the same quantities. Bring to the boil and boil for about thirty minutes. Test for setting then pot as usual.

J
E
L
L
I
E
S

Apple, Blackberry & Elderberry Jelly

1 kilo/2lbs cooking apples
500g/1lb blackberries
500g/1lb elderberries
A handful of sloes

Follow the same recipe as above.

Gooseberry Mint Jelly

1.5 kilos/3lbs green gooseberries
1 lemon
Sugar
Fresh mint

Put the cleaned gooseberries in a pan with the lemon juice. Just cover with water and simmer to a pulp. Strain and finish as for mint jelly but add a bunch of slightly bruised mint with the sugar. When setting point is reached, remove the mint and pot in the usual way.

Jams

Jersey French   *consèrve* (f)
Guernsey French   *d'la g'laïe*

Raspberry Jam

This recipe comes from La Société Guernesiase.

560g/18oz sugar to every pound of raspberries
Press the raspberries, almost to a pulp, in a bowl. Cover with sugar then leave for thirty-six to forty-eight hours. Tip into a pan and slowly bring to the boil stirring all the time. Once boiling hard, remove from the heat, remove any scum. Pot while it is hot.

Rhubarb & Ginger Jam

1.5kilos/3lbs rhubarb   3 lemons
1.5kilos/3lbs sugar   90g/3oz crystallised ginger

Trim the washed rhubarb and cut into small chunks. Alternate the rhubarb and sugar in layers in a bowl. Pour over the lemon juice. Leave for eight hours. Place the rhubarb and sugar in a pan. Add the finely chopped crystallised ginger. Boil rapidly for about twenty-thirty minutes. Test for setting. Pot in the usual way.

Apple & Ginger Jam

                                 60g/2oz ground ginger
3kilos/6lbs cooking apples   250g/8oz preserved ginger
2.5kilos/5lbs sugar   3 lemons

Tie the apple peel, cores and bruised ginger into a piece of muslin. Put the apple peel and cores into a cloth or muslin bag. Put the sliced apples and bag in a pan. Add the water, ground ginger, grated rind and juice of the lemons. Simmer for about fifteen minutes. Remove the bag, add the finely chopped ginger and sugar. When the sugar has dissolved, boil rapidly for about twenty minutes. Test for setting. Pot in the usual way.

Black Butter
Jersey French   *beurre* (f) *nièr*

As mentioned on page 107, the annual making of Black Butter – a conserve made from apples and cider – was a major event in Jersey in times past. Now, only a few enthusiasts continue the tradition. Nan du Feu tells me that the butter gets so thick that only men are strong enough to stir it, to keep it from burning. They used a strong wooden implement – rather like a large hoe which had a long handle and was called a *rabot*. Nan tells me how she recently attended a very cheerful re-enactment at a Methodist school room. The occasion was a fund-raising event to benefit the Church and other good causes. Nan was impressed by the laughter and gossip of those involved as well as the sight of so many barrels filled with peeled apples awaiting cooking in the huge *bashin* – an antique brass pan.

B
E
V
E
R
A
G
E
S

One recipe in the W.I. booklet *Bouon Appétit* suggests 20 cabots which is 700lbs of apples – no wonder it was a communal activity!

This recipe from the same booklet is easier to handle for those wishing to continue the Black Butter tradition:

'2.5 kilos/5lbs sweet apples
1kilo/2lbs sour apples
4litres/8 pints cider
5 kilos/10lbs white sugar
4 lemons
1 dessert spoon mixed spice
Half stick liquorice (optional)

Boil the cider until reduced to half. Gradually add the peeled, cored and sliced sweet apples. Add the liquorice and minced lemons. When bubbling, add the peeled, cored and sliced sour apples. Cook until thick, then add the sugar, stirring frequently. When very thick and dark, add the spice. Pot in the usual way.'

I used the above recipe but reduced the amount of sugar to 1 kilo/ 2lbs. I made it in a preseving pan. Once it was bubbling, I put it in the oven where it stayed for about thirty-six hours. Occasionally I stirred it and each time I noticed it was getting blacker until it was reduced to a thick dark consistency, resembling chutney. I also noticed that each time I lifted the lid from the pan, I seemed to inhale Christmas pudding! Once potted, I put it in a cool place to mature for a few weeks before using.

Beverages

Sloe Gin

With a needle, prick the sloes in several places and put them in an empty glass bottle. Trickle granulated sugar to cover the sloes. Fill with gin. Seal securely and leave for at least three months, the longer the better. Some people make it one year for the next.

B
E
V
E
R
A
G
E
S

Blackberry Brandy

2kilos/4lbs blackberries
250g/8oz sugar
1 litre bottle brandy

Share the blackberries between two screw-top glass glass bottles or one kilner jar. Add the sugar and brandy. Seal or firmly screw the top. Shake every few days until the sugar has dissolved. Place in a dark cupboard. Gently shake every couple of weeks then after three months, strain and bottle the juice. Keep for as long as possible before drinking, although it is just ready for Christmas!

Milk Punch

This is an old recipe from La Société Guernesiaise. I haven't tried it but imagine it must be very good – it sounds awesome.

16 fine lemons
1.5kilos/3lbs sugar lumps
4 Seville oranges
3 bottles rum
1 bottle French brandy

1 bottle old Madeira
3quarts – 3litres/6 pints boiling water
1/2 drachm grated nutmeg
120g/4ozs cinnamon
3 pints/1.5 litres new milk

Rub the sugar lumps on the lemons and oranges to extract essence from the peel. Squeeze the fruit and strain the juice. Put the sugar and juice into an earthen pan and pour the boiling water over it. Take a quart – 1litre/2pint – jug in each hand, dip out the liquid and pour it back rapidly, holding jugs as high as possible. Do this for twenty minutes, then add the spirit and the wine a bottle at a time and continue the mixing process until the punch has a smooth soft flavour which will take three-quarters of an hour. Boil the spice in the milk and pour into the punch. Stir it once quickly then cover the pan with an earthen lid and a thick cover over that and let it remain undisturbed for eight hours. Strain it through flannel about three times if not bright. Put it into bottles and cork it securely. It improves by keeping.

B
E
V
E
R
A
G
E
S

Blackberry Syrup

This is excellent for sore throats and children love it.

2 kilos/4lbs blackberries　　　550ml/20fl oz water
1 lemon　　　　　　　　　　granulated sugar

Simmer the blackberries in the water and lemon juice until soft and pulpy. Lay a cloth across a colander or use a muslin bag to strain the juice into a bowl. Measure the juice and to each 550ml/20fl oz, add 375g/12oz of sugar. Gently heat, stirring all the time until the sugar has dissolved, then simmer until syrupy. As it boils, remove any scum with a spoon. Cool a little, then fill glass bottles with screw tops or corks.

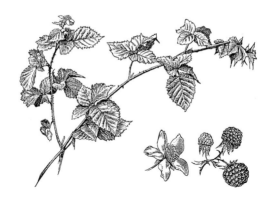

Winter

| Jersey French | *l'hivé* (m) |
| Guernsey French | *l'hivé* (m) |

December ~ January ~ February

Winter is the coldest season, a time of inactivity when growth ceases. By November we have become accustomed to the shorter days and the drop in temperature. However, there is always something to celebrate with the run up to Christmas and New Year.

In the past, an important occasion in mid-December was the annual Fat Stock Show which was held in Guernsey. Competition was keen as it was prestigious to be awarded the coveted winner's rosette. After judging, the animals were paraded as they made their melancholy journey to the slaughter-house.

Bob Chilcott, whose family had a presence in the market for generations, tells me that he remembers accompanying his father on a visit to a Mr Brehaut at Les Sages in Guernsey during the first week of December. Mr Brehaut's animals were regular winners at the Christmas Fat Stock shows; on this occasion there were two steers which had been specially fattened since mid-October. These beasts had been fed entirely on parsnips and turnips so that the air in the stable was fetid with the smell of the roots and animal sweat! From Les Sages, the Chilcotts made their way to a farmer in the King's Mills who specialised in fattening heifers in the belief these produced sweeter meat.

Butchers vied with one another to have the champion carcass to display on their stalls as there would be an enthusiastic demand for this meat. A local butcher told me that that the beef looked like a 'sea of yellow' from the yellow fat of the local beef animals. Bob recounted how, while training at the great

London meat market of Smithfields, he arranged the purchase of a prize bullock for display on his father's Christmas stall. Imagine Bob's dismay when his father refused to give this particular carcass pride of place. Mystified, Bob learned that, because of its white fat, few people would entertain buying the meat! How tastes change!

Because of the lack of cold storage, butchers generally hung their sides of beef on their shop fronts and it was not unusual for them to remain there for a week or even more but then it was, of course, winter. This enforced hanging helped the beef improve as time went on.

Bob well remembers how the Markets looked at Christmas in St Peter Port fifty years ago – hives of activity and without piped music either! In the Meat Market turkeys, geese, pheasants with other poultry, some still feathered, hung alongside huge sides of beef and pork. In the Fish Market were splendid displays of fish and shellfish with baskets of eggs and butter pats finding their way there too. The Fruit and Vegetable Market offered colourful displays of both fruit and vegetables but being Christmas, with the addition of boxes of dates, threaded rings of figs, nuts and oranges and lemons, to name just a few. Oranges were a particular treat, something to be put in most children's stockings on Christmas Eve.

Sadly today, in St Peter Port, with the Markets awaiting redevelopment, nearly all the traders have gone and they are but a shadow of their former glory. Happily, the St Helier Markets remain much as they were, lively and vibrant with no shortage of stall-holders.

Christmas and New Year have always been times for seeing family and friends, the exchange of gifts and gossip and, of course, feasting. Christmas festivities continue unabated to this day although the 'high teas' of yesteryear have mainly given way to Christmas Lunch or Dinner. I well remember tea time Christmas visits to relations during the 1950s, when the table would be fairly groaning with good things to eat. It was important, socially, to offer generously and of the best quality; as a result great care was taken over the meal. The table was laden with plates of cold ham and beef, bread and butter, pickles and chutneys. On the sideboard were fruit flans, trifle, gâche, seed cake and Victoria sponge cakes – protests were ignored and your plate would be filled time and time again!

In the past, especially in the country, December 23rd was known as *La Longue Veille*. Loosely translated, it means the 'long eve'. It was a time for the final preparation of goods for the Market and the completion of knitting which would also be offered for sale. Work would be done to the sound of music and songs, as it was a time to be enjoyed. The tradition was to offer sandwiches, tea and cider with squares of apple pie, *ent'e daëux craoutes* (between two layers of pastry), *galaettes* and *gâche.*

In recent years, my niece and her husband have revived the old *Longue Veille* custom. It's a lively, traditional, evening with much merriment although, it must be said, no longer are there any goods being prepared for market!

The following day, being Christmas Eve, men, women and children were up bright and early to make the journey into town to sell their goods, to visit the Markets or just for the outing. There was an air of anticipation.

Christmas Day was spent quietly. The religious significance of the Feast was extremely important and the exchange of gifts was far more modest compared with current standards. Back from church or chapel the family would sit down to a roast of beef or perhaps chicken, followed by plum pudding. It wasn't until the twentieth century that turkey started to appear on the menu along with crackers on the festive table.

January heralded the beginning of the ploughing season which, until the late 1700s, had been carried out by hand.

Farmers and helpers, horses and oxen would gather for a cooperative effort in ploughing. In Guernsey, this was called *La Grand Tcherue* while in Jersey, it was *La Grand Tchethue*. There were many types of ploughs but *La Grand,* the 'Big One' was used for ploughing deep furrows in larger fields. Anything from two to ten bullocks and six to eight horses were harnessed up to the 'Big One' and much skill was needed to control both animals and plough. This event was also a social occasion with many families, neighbours and friends taking part. At the end of each day of ploughing all would sit down for a meal which would include cabbage soup, beef and pork (boiled or roasted) and potatoes, followed by cake such as *gâche a corinte* (currant cake) washed down with copious amounts of tea or cider.

At the other end of the scale, the smaller fields and the *côtils* continued to be prepared for planting by hand or perhaps with the help of a small plough pulled by just one horse.

The days of *La Grand Tcherue/Tchethue* inevitably came to an end with the arrival of mechanisation towards the end of the nineteenth century.

As the soil was being prepared an eye was kept on seed potatoes, watching for the first signs of sprouting. Once the soil had warmed a little the planting of potatoes was followed by parsnips and other vegetables would start.

By December the emphasis is on robust meals to keep bodies warm and coughs and colds at bay.

ELEVENTH MONTH **NOVEMBER** THIRTY DAYS

Beef

Jersey French	*viande* (f), *dé vaque*
Guernsey French	*boeu* (in the high parishes)
	boeuf (in the lower parishes)

Channel Islands' cows are dairy cattle bred for their milk so rich in butterfat. Some steers and heifers would be fattened for Christmas and other special occasions. These and other cattle were slaughtered but pork was the everyday meat.

Spiced Beef

This is an excellent way of preparing beef for the festive season as it can be done well in advance and once cooked will keep for at least two weeks. It can be sliced thinly, sits happily beside cold ham and is very good with pickles and chutneys, mashed potato and many salads

Initial Preparation

3 kilo/6lb piece of topside or silverside
3 cloves garlic

60g/2oz brown sugar	500g/1lb salt
Spice Mixture	Cooking Stock
4-5 bay leaves	3 carrots
1 tsp ground cloves	3 onions
1 tsp grated nutmeg	A handful of herbs, such as thyme,
1 tsp ground black pepper	rosemary, sage, savory or marjoram

Wash and trim the beef, removing any bits of gristle. It will probably need shaping so roll and tie it into an oblong. Rub it with the sugar. Peel the garlic and insert slivers at random. Leave for about three hours.

Next, mix the ground spices with the salt and rub it into the beef making sure it gets everywhere. Place the meat in a glass or plastic

M
E
A
T

bowl with the bay leaves. Cover with a cloth. Leave in a very cold place, turning and spooning the salty spice mixture over the beef twice a day for seven days. You will notice that it seems to shrink daily but this is because the salt is drawing the moisture out and the flesh is becoming firmer.

In a pan large enough to comfortably hold the beef, place the sliced carrots, onions and herbs. Rinse the beef and place in the pan. Cover with water and simmer for five hours, topping up with water if necessary.

Remove the beef from the pan and place between two plates, chopping boards, or small planks of wood. Place a heavy weight on top and leave in a cold place overnight.

It is then ready to serve but a glaze of aspic jelly adds a really professional touch!

Casserole of Beef in Beer

Serves 4

1 kilo/2lbs lean stewing beef
120g/4oz piece of bacon
250g/8oz mushrooms
250g/8oz chopped tomatoes
1 onion

3-4 bay leaves
2 cloves garlic
Herbs such as thyme and rosemary
Salt and pepper

For the marinade

2 tbsp olive oil
275 ml/10fl oz beer
2 tbsp red wine vinegar
1 chopped carrot, 1 chopped
   onion, 2-3 stalks celery
2 bay leaves
A few sprigs of thyme
Salt and pepper

Make the marinade by frying the vegetables in the olive oil till browned. Add the remaining ingredients. Simmer gently for about thirty minutes and then allow to cool.

Meanwhile, cut the meat into pieces and place in a bowl. Pour the cooled marinade over the beef and leave for about twenty-four hours, turning occasionally.

Drain the beef but keep the marinade. Dice the bacon and fry in a little olive oil along with the sliced onion and garlic. Place in an ovenproof casserole. Next fry the mushrooms and add to the casserole. Now fry the beef until browned and any liquid has evaporated. Add the beef to the casserole along with the herbs, bay leaf and chopped tomatoes. Pour over the marinade. Season. Cook slowly in a moderate oven for about three hours until the meat is tender. Make sure it doesn't dry out by adding more liquid.

A serving suggestion is mashed potatoes or buttered noodles and purple sprouting broccoli.

MEAT

Boiled Beef & Carrots

Boiled beef remains a popular and economical dish and, at this time of year, the root vegetables to accompany it are at their best. Nice, light dumplings also go wonderfully well with boiled beef and carrots.

Serves 4
1 kilo/2lb piece of silverside, flank or topside
500g/1lb carrots   2 small turnips (about 250g/8oz)
2 onions   Several sprigs of thyme or 1 tsp dried thyme
Salt and pepper

Chop the vegetables and place in a roomy pan or cast-iron casserole with the herbs, salt and pepper. Cover with water and bring to the boil. Tie the beef into a round and put it in with the vegetables. Cook in a moderate oven 190°C, 375°F, Gas 5 for two hours. It may be necessary to remove any scum after about twenty minutes of cooking.

Dumplings
120g/4oz plain flour
1 level tsp baking powder
60g/2oz shredded suet
1 tbsp chopped parsley
Salt and pepper
Water to mix

Place the seasoned flour, suet, baking powder and chopped parsley in a roomy bowl.

Mix to a sticky dough with water.

With floured hands, roll the dough into eight or nine small balls.

Before cooking them, remove the meat and some of the vegetables from the casserole as this will allow more room for the dumplings. Keep both warm.

Poach the dumplings for about ten minutes.

Serve the meat surrounded by the vegetables and dumplings with the cooking liquor poured over.

Steak & Kidney Pudding

Serves 6
1 kilo/2lbs lean stewing steak
500g/1lb beef kidney
1 onion
120g/4oz mushrooms
Flour for coating
60g/2oz butter

Suet Crust Pastry
To line a 1 litre/2 pint pudding
  basin
300g/10oz plain flour
120g/4oz suet
2 heaped tsp baking powder
5-6 tbsp tepid water
Salt and pepper

MEAT

I recommend cooking the meats first. This can be done the day before.

Chop the onions and quarter the mushrooms, frying both in the butter. Remove from the pan and fry the floured cubed beef and kidney. Add the mushrooms and onion to the meat, cover with water, season it and cook gently in the pan or in a casserole until tender. Allow to cool and then refrigerate until needed.

To make the pastry, sieve the flour and baking powder. Add the suet, salt and pepper. Mix to a slightly tacky dough that isn't too wet or too dry. Knead the dough quickly and gently to form a ball. Use a third for the lid and the rest to line the bowl.

Put the meat mixture into the pastry lined bowl. Add water or stock to come three-quarters of the way up. Damp the edge and add the lid. Cover with a pleated piece of greaseproof (to allow for swelling) and tie down. Cover with foil, tying securely. Using a steamer or, placing a trivet in a saucepan with water coming two-thirds up the side of the bowl, simmer gently for one and a half to two hours.

Serve immediately. Traditionally, a white cloth is tied around the bowl.

For thousands of years the Spice Routes have brought spices to the West – perhaps the earliest example of 'Food Miles'. Certainly, before refrigeration, spices were very necessary to disguise the strong smell and flavour of foods which were probably well past their sell-by dates. Not only that, but spices introduced a whole range of exotic flavours which found ready acceptance among western palates.

Curry is an oriental, chiefly Indian, combination of spices, normally including chilli, which has been popular in Europe, even before Clive of India and the days of the Raj.

M
E
A
T

It was, therefore, no surprise to come across the following recipe for curry powder in the booklet of ninteenth century recipes, *Guernsey Dishes of Bygone Days*, assembled by J. Stevens-Cox:

'RECIPE FOR GENUINE CURRY POWDER

Coriander seed: 3oz
Turmeric: 3oz
Black Pepper: 1oz
White Mustard seed: 1oz
Best Jamaica ginger: 1oz

Allspice: half oz
Jessen Cardomons (1): half oz
Cummin Seed: quarter oz
Fenngreek seed (2): quarter oz
Cayenne pepper: quarter oz'

Be sure all ingredients are fresh and of best quality. Finely powder the whole mix and sift. Keep closely corked and dry. This mixture will make a dozen curries. This suscitating oriental stimulant was brought to England from India c.1800 and was quickly passed among those families who delight with Gastronomy.'

I made a lamb curry using the above curry powder. It was very pleasant but lacked the bite of chilli.

Curried Beef

Serves 4
750g/1.5lbs stewing beef
1 onion
1 clove garlic
1 small chilli with seeds removed
1 tbsp oil
2-3 tbsp Madras curry powder or 2 tbsp curry paste
  (add more to be really hot)

1 tbsp tomato purée or 2-3
  fresh tomatoes
Juice of half a lemon
150ml/5oz coconut milk
Salt and pepper

Fry the onion and chopped garlic in the oil until soft then put in an ovenproof casserole. In the same pan fry the trimmed and cubed meat until dry and brown. Add the curry powder or paste, tomato purée or chopped tomatoes, chopped chilli and lemon juice. Season. Cover with water and a lid and cook in a moderate oven for at least an hour. Just before serving, add the coconut milk and check seasoning. Serve with boiled rice, poppadoms, chutney and other small dishes of your choice, such as raita, chopped raw onion and tomato, dried toasted coconut and so on.

At this time of the year, the weeding out of older birds takes place. Young, strong birds are kept as they will be needed for sitting on eggs to hatch out the next generation.

Chicken

Jersey French	*pouochîn*(m), *poulet* (m)
Guernsey French	*pouchin* (m) (lower parishes)
	pouachin (m) (higher parishes)

Chicken as a meat is known as *du poulet*

Chickens were probably one of the first animals to be domesticated, the value of their flesh and eggs having long been appreciated. By the mid-1960s, growing demand for chicken and eggs led to the development of large-scale, intensive chicken farming. Eventually, considerations of animal cruelty and public health concerns led to something of a rebellion against mass-produced and increasingly tasteless chicken. Government intervention has hopefully eliminated the worst excesses and, coupled with the public outcry, there has been a welcome return to free-range, organic as well as specialist, production. Buy the best you can afford.

Casserole of Chicken

Serves 4

1 chicken weighing about 1.5kilos/3lbs cut into portions

120g/4oz butter	1 crushed clove garlic
15/20 small onions	275 ml/half pint red wine
250g/8oz button mushrooms	Flour for dusting the chicken
120g/4oz streaky bacon	Salt and pepper

In a frying pan, melt half the butter and fry the floured chicken portions until golden brown. Put them in an oven-proof casserole. In the same pan, fry the onions and garlic in the other half of butter, then the button mushrooms and finally the chopped bacon. Add them to the chicken. Pour over the red wine and a little extra water. Season with salt and pepper and cook at 190°C, 375°F, Gas 5 for between an hour and an hour and a half.

Check to make sure that it doesn't dry out.

POULTRY

Boiled Fowl

This traditional recipe may not appeal to those accustomed to crisp, golden roast chicken; however, boiled chicken is actually very tasty and, of course, moist. The cooking liquor helps to make a particularly good parsley sauce to go with it.

Serves 6
1 medium sized chicken 1-1.5 kilos or 2-3 lbs
2-3 carrots
2 onions spiked with cloves
2-3 potatoes
2 small turnips
Fresh herbs such as sage, rosemary, thyme or 1 tsp mixed dried herbs
Salt and pepper

If necessary tie the chicken into shape and put it in a roomy ovenproof casserole or saucepan.

Add the diced vegetables and fresh or dried herbs. Season. Cover with water and bring slowly to the boil, reducing the heat so that it just barely simmers. Cook for about one hour until tender.

Melt 30g/1oz butter in a pan, stir in 1 tbsp flour and mix well. Gently add sufficient cooking liquor to produce a thickish sauce. Stirring, bring to the boil. If it is too thick, add a little more cooking liquor. Check seasoning, add two tbsp chopped parsley.

Serve the chicken on a dish. Surround it with the vegetables with the sauce carefully poured over.

Goose

| Jersey French | *ouaie* (f) |
| Guernsey French | *ouaie* (f) |

Goose was another indispensable bird around the farm, not only to keep prowlers at bay but to provide meat and grease.

Why is goose fat called grease? No doubt because that was and still is one of its many uses – greasing. It was the only grease allowed in the dairy to keep the cogs on the butter churn running sweetly. Animals' hooves were greased with it to prevent them cracking and harness was greased to keep it soft and pliable.

Other uses were as a spread, on bread, having been mixed with chopped parsley and onion. It was also used in poultices to ease painful chests and has waterproofing properties.

Geese reared for the table are plump with a very distinct, succulent flavour. They are ready for eating at one year-old.

Roast Goose with Mushroom Stuffing

As goose tends to be a fatty bird, it is best to place your bird on a rack in the oven with a tray underneath, to try to catch the drips and in which you can also roast the potatoes, parsnips, onions, etc. You may have to clean the oven but you will achieve a better tasting and healthier result.

A 4 kilo/8lb bird provides 6-8 helpings.

Roast for two and a half hours starting in an oven at 215°C, 425°F, Gas 7 for thirty minutes then reduce the temperature to 200°C, 400°F, Gas 6.

A 6kilo/12lb bird provides 8-10 helpings and should be roasted in the same way for about three and a quarter hours.

Baste regularly, covering the breast with foil when it is golden brown.

Traditional accompaniments are apple sauce, bread sauce, roast and

P
O
U
L
T
R
Y

boiled potatoes, a stuffing of sage and onion or forcemeat balls.

Mushroom Stuffing
500g/8oz chopped button mushrooms
1 tbsp chopped parsley and onion
120g/4oz breadcrumbs
6og/2oz chopped bacon
1 egg
Seasoning

All are mixed together to fill the cavity of the goose with an onion or apple in the opening to prevent the stuffing coming out. Tying the legs will also keep the goose in shape.

Save the goose grease. It is the best for roasting or frying vegetables for weeks to come!

It is generally acknowledged that most fish, including shellfish, is at its best during the winter months. January also sees the start of the ormer gathering tides, when the hardy enthusiasts pursue their prey – up to their waists in water – at the coldest time of year.

F
I
S
H

Crab

| Jersey French | *crabe* (f), *chancre* (m), *houais* (m) |
| Guernsey French | *crabe* or *chancresse* (f), *chancre* (m) |

What can I say about crab except that it is, for me, the most delicious shellfish found in our waters. I have tasted crab elsewhere but it is never as good as ours.

The best way of eating crab is freshly picked with as little adornment as possible. But there are times when it is good to have a change.

Crab cakes with Coriander

I have a feeling of guilt when using crabmeat to make a hot dish but these crab cakes are very tasty and can be prepared in advance. They are also a good way of stretching any left-over crabmeat.

Serves 4

500g/1lb crabmeat	2 egg yolks
90g/3oz breadcrumbs	Tabasco
1 small onion	1 tbsp chopped parsley & coriander
60g/2oz butter	Seasoning
1 lemon	Oil or butter for frying

Fry the chopped onion in butter till soft. Remove from the heat.

In a bowl, place the crabmeat, breadcrumbs, cooled onion, egg yolks, lemon juice and chopped herbs. Season with salt and pepper and tabasco.

Shape into eight cakes. Place on a plate and refrigerate for at least two hours.

Fry in butter or oil. Don't turn until a crust has formed underneath as they are delicate and don't enjoy too much turning, once is enough!

Serve on four plates garnished with a little watercress or salad leaves.

F
I
S
H

Oysters

Jersey French	hître (f)
Guernseysey french	huitre (f)

In the past oysters were plentiful in Island waters but this is no longer the case. As a result, some commercial oyster farming takes place locally but most of the oysters now eaten in the Islands come from France or England.

Oysters the Classic Way

A good guide is approximately six oysters per person.

Open them at home as it is important to keep the juices within the shell. Opening them can be difficult and there is a knack. What is most important is to protect the hand holding the oyster with a glove or towel and to use the proper short bladed knife with the protective guard. Oyster shell can give a nasty cut, often difficult to heal.

Prepare a large or individual plates with crushed ice and if possible some seaweed as this helps to stabilise the oysters and gives a sense of 'occasion'.

Place the opened oysters radiating from the centre with half a lemon in the middle.

Fifteen minutes should be sufficient to chill them.

Oysters in a Cream Sauce

Serves 4

Butter for greasing
20 oysters
275ml/10fl oz double cream
8tbsp white breadcrumbs

2 tbsp chopped parsley
3 ripe tomatoes
Salt and cayenne pepper

Shuck the oysters but keep the liquid.

Butter four ovenproof dishes. Mix the parsley with the breadcrumbs and scatter half over the bottom of the dishes. Peel and chop the tomatoes using only the flesh and sprinkle over the breadcrumbs.

Place five oysters in each dish, dust with salt and cayenne pepper. Add the other half of breadcrumb mixture. Add the liquid from the oysters to the cream and pour into each dish.

Bake in a medium oven for ten minutes.

Shellfish Platter

This can be a dish for a festive occasion and can be as simple or extravagant as you wish. In the islands we have the added advantage of being able to go to the beach to gather seaweed as a base for the shellfish.

The assortment can consist of crab, oysters, cooked mussels, prawns, langoustine, shrimps even limpets.

How much per person? Appetites of course vary but a rule of thumb, for each person could be some or all of the following: half a small crab, four oysters, six mussels, two or three langoustine, six prawns and a scattering of shrimp and winkles.

This seafood platter, beautifully arranged on its bed of seaweed and with a scattering of lemon wedges, a bowl of home-made mayonnaise alongside, truly is a feast for the Gods. And don't forget a good Muscadet or other dry white wine to wash it down.

Red Mullet

Jersey French	*mulet rouage* (m)
Guernsey French	*rouget mulet* (m) or *rouge molet* (m)

Red mullet is excellent from October until March. It is a heavily scaled fish but can be cooked unscaled which helps to keep in the juices. However, I think it better to scale mullet before cooking and this is quite easy. Alternatively, ask your fishmonger to do it.

It is a good fish to cook whole - simply make a couple of diagonal cuts on one side and push in a little butter and a squeeze of lemon juice. After seasoning with salt and pepper just fry, bake or grill.

When cooked whole in this way, the fish may be enjoyed either hot or cold.

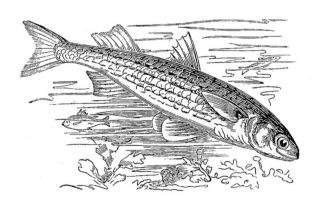

Skate/Ray

Jersey French	*raie* (f) or *cârée* (f)
Guernsey French	*d'la raie* (f) – blonde or mottled
	grison (m) – grey ray

This large flat fish comes into its own during the cooler months. It has always been a popular fish and I was surprised to learn that it is often used in fish and chip shops. Ray is a fish that needs to relax to develop. Herbert Nicholls, a retired fisherman tells me that having caught one, he would wait until the next day to sell it.

Ray with Black Butter

Serves 4

4 wing pieces preferably from towards the centre of the body as they are thicker and meatier. Each piece weighing about 250g /6oz.

90g/3oz butter
1 lemon
1 tbsp capers
1 tbsp chopped parsley
2 tbsp white wine vinegar
Salt and pepper

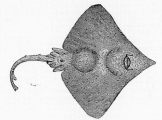

Place the pieces of skate in a large pan and pour over the vinegar, lemon juice and a little water. Season with salt and pepper. Cover with foil and bring slowly to the boil, simmer for about fifteen minutes. Alternatively, cook in a fairly hot oven for fifteen to twenty minutes.

Carefully lift from the poaching water and place on a serving plate. Cover with the foil and keep warm.

Place the butter in a small pan, cook until it begins to turn brown. Don't allow the butter to become too black otherwise it will taste burnt and bitter.

Add the capers and chopped parsley and swirling it around and, if necessary, some of the cooking liquor. Pour over the skate pieces

F
I
S
H

Smoking is the traditional way to semi-preserve haddock. Doing so imparts its characteristic flavour. Dyed 'smoked' haddock is also available. This is cheaper but not so good.

Smoked Haddock Soufflé

Serves 4
375g/12oz smoked haddock
60g/2oz butter & extra for buttering
Salt and cayenne pepper

2 tbsp chopped parsley
300ml/10fl oz milk
30g/1oz plain flour
4 eggs

Place the washed haddock in a pan with the milk. Cover and simmer for ten minutes. Remove the fish and keep the cooking liquid. When cool enough to handle, remove and flake the flesh, discarding the skin and any bones.

In a pan, melt the butter and blend in the flour.

Gradually add the milk to make a thick creamy sauce, add a little water if the sauce is too thick. Season with cayenne pepper and a little salt. Add the flaked fish, egg yolks and parsley, stirring it in thoroughly. Whisk the egg whites and fold them into the mixture. Turn into a well buttered soufflé dish and bake at 200°C, 400°F, Gas 6 for about thirty minutes.

Smoked Haddock with a Mustard Sauce

2 fillets weighing about 1kilo/2lbs smoked haddock
425ml/15fl oz milk
1 onion
2 bay leaves
30g/1oz butter

30g/1oz flour
6 cloves
1 tbsp English mustard
Salt and pepper

Cut the fillets in two. Put the milk, sliced onion, bay leaves and cloves in a pan or ovenproof dish. Lay the fish flesh side down. Poach or cook in a preheated moderate oven for fifteen minutes. Remove from the cooking liquor and keep warm. In a small pan, melt the butter, add the flour and mustard. Gradually add the cooking liquor until it thickens. Check seasoning then pour it over the fish.

Parsnip

Jersey French	*paînfais* (f), *bênarde* (f)
Guernsey French	*pônais* (f)

The parsnip has played an important role in the islands for at least four hundred years. It fed both man and beast, ensuring survival through the winter. The seeds were sown in deep trenches in March to grow and mature throughout the year until it was time to plough the land again. They were left in the ground all the time, surviving even the worst frost. Having prepared the soil and sown the seed there was more work to come as, once the young seedlings began to appear, it was necessary to weed them. Gangs of men on their hands and knees worked up and down the rows. Even after the introduction of the hoe some still preferred the old way of getting down to it.

Steers and pigs were fattened on parsnips in readiness for the Christmas market. A steer could eat over a hundredweight every day. Parsnips were never washed as it was considered that removed some of the flavour; they were cut vertically to prevent the animal choking.

I can remember my Mother saying that when she bought a piece of pork she knew if the pig had been fed on parsnips as the meat had a special sweetness.

My favourite way of cooking parsnips is to parboil them for five minutes, then to roast them around the joint. Alternatively roasted in butter or oil. Another very good way of cooking them is as chips. Cut the parsnip in half unless it is really big, then cut it into three. Standing it on end, cut it into quarters and cut those into chip size fingers. Put them in a pan of cold water, bring to the boil and cook for two to three minutes. Drain, dry in a cloth and cook as they are in hot oil. Alternatively, they can be tossed in flour before cooking. Sprinkle with salt on serving.

Panais à la Graisse

Parsnips and potatoes were sliced into a roasting pan with just enough water to cover them. On top was put a piece of meat, usually pork or a piece of smoked ham cut from the side on the rack.

V
E
G
E
T
A
B
L
E
S

Seasoning was added and on top a suet crust. This was gently simmered for three to four hours.

I have tried a variation of this recipe with a piece of smoked ham cut into small pieces. I cooked it in a pan until everything was soft and browned. I didn't put on a pastry lid but it was really good and easily done.

Parsnip & Apple Soup

Serves 4

500g/1lb parsnips
125g/4oz apple that has been
   peeled, cored and chopped
45g/1.5oz butter
1 medium onion
1 clove garlic
1 dessertspoon curry powder
1 litre/2 pints chicken or vegetable stock

Half lemon
1 small potato
2 tbsp double cream
Salt and pepper
Chopped chives or parsley
   for garnishing

In a roomy pan, fry the chopped onion and garlic in the butter. Add the chopped parsnip, apple, potato and fry for a further five minutes. Add the curry powder, stock and lemon juice.

Season and simmer for about thirty minutes. Liquidise until smooth. Reheat and when hot swirl in the cream and scatter with chopped chives or parsley.

Parsnip & Apple Cakes

Serves 4

2 medium parsnips
2 medium eating apples
2 shallots

1 tbsp parsley
Salt and pepper
Butter or dripping for frying
1 egg

These are quite rough to look at and in texture but very good to eat. Peel and dice the parsnip. Boil in a little salted water for five minutes then add the peeled and diced apple for a further five minutes. Meanwhile, fry the finely chopped shallots in a little of the butter. Drain the parsnip and apple. Put back in the saucepan, shaking to get rid of any excess water. Mash then add the shallot, beaten egg, parsley and seasoning. Mix all together then shape into eight cakes. Refrigerate them for at least two hours, then fry in the butter or dripping.

Potatoes

Jersey French	*patate* (f)
Guernsey French	*patate* (f)

Understandably, the famous Jersey Royal – the 'king' of early potatoes grown in Jersey – is described, in some detail, in the Spring section (page 39). Many other main crop varieties are, of course, grown in the Islands for use when a more substantial potato is needed, such as during the winter. Chipped, boiled, roast or mashed – each method has its moment. And what could be more warming, in winter, than a bowl of potato soup? Potato is more satisfying than rice or noodles and it is difficult to imagine a roast being served with anything other than roast potatoes.

Potatoes generally fall into two categories – floury and waxy. Floury varieties are particularly good for mashing and waxy ones are favoured when you don't want the potato to collapse.

Layered potatoes with cream

Serves 6
Approx. 1 kg/2lbs waxy potatoes
2 shallots
225ml/10fl oz double cream
225ml/10fl oz creamy milk
Salt and black pepper
Butter for greasing the dish
Grated nutmeg

Peel and slice the potatoes into a buttered ovenproof dish. Finely chop the shallots and scatter over. Mix the cream and milk, seasoning with salt and plenty of freshly ground black pepper. Pour over the potatoes finishing off with grated nutmeg.
Cover and cook in a moderate oven, 200°C, 400°F, Gas 6 for one hour reducing the heat for a further thirty minutes.

VEGETABLES

Potato & Leek Soup

Serves 4

1 medium onion	2 tbsp double cream
2 leeks	Salt and pepper
500g/1lb potatoes	1 tbsp chopped parsley or chives
60g/2oz butter	2 or 3 sprigs of thyme
1 litre/40fl oz chicken stock or 2 stock cubes	

In a roomy pan gently fry the chopped onion in the butter. Add the sliced leek and potato cut into chunks. Turn in the butter for a further 5 minutes. Add the stock, thyme and seasoning and simmer for about an hour. Either whizz the soup in a blender or pass it through the mouli. Check seasoning. When ready to serve, bring to boiling point and off the heat, stir in the cream and sprinkle with the chopped parsley or chives.

Mixed Vegetable Soup

This can be made with a variety of vegetables including haricot beans. I can remember that my Grandmother always had a pot of soup on the go and every day more vegetables were added or sometimes a tin of cream of tomato soup. She would use tomatoes, parsnips, carrots, leeks, turnips, swede, celery, potatoes and onions with a handful of herbs thrown in for good luck.

Serves 4

1 large or 2 small carrots	1 litre meat or vegetable stock
1 onion	or 2 stock cubes
2/3 sticks celery	3-4 sprigs thyme
90g/3oz haricot beans	60g/2oz butter or 1 tbsp dripping
4/5 florets of cauliflower	Salt and pepper

Soak the haricot beans overnight.
Fry the chopped onion until soft. Add the rinsed haricot beans, chopped celery, carrot, stock, sprigs of thyme and seasoning. Simmer for an hour until the haricots are cooked then add the florets of cauliflower and simmer for a further fifteen minutes. Serve piping hot.

Swede/Turnip

Jersey French	*suidiche, navet* (m)
Guernsey French	*suède* (m), *aen navet d'suède* (m)

Like the parsnip, the swede is also enjoying a revival. It grows well in the islands as we don't have the really hard frosts that cause damage. It is used as winter fodder for cattle. A garden variety is used in the kitchen but don't choose ones that are too big or old as the older they are, the ranker the flavour. The delicate yellow orange colour intensifies on cooking.

Swede boiled then mashed with butter and salt with lots of pepper is my favourite way of serving it.

It can be cut into cubes and cooked in boiling water for two to three minutes then drained. Fry in butter until browned finally adding a few shreds of fresh ginger.

Brussels Sprouts

| Jersey French | *cabochaons* (m pl) |
| Guernsey French | *P'tits chaoux* (m pl) |

Although sprouts are available from September through to March, I like to consider them as a winter vegetable – certainly by the end of February they are past their prime.

Sprouts need care when cooking. It is rather like cooking a miniature cabbage. Steaming takes about ten minutes whereas boiling takes about five. Once cooked they need to be served straight away or they will lose their crispness and colour. Accompaniments that go well are crisply fried pieces of bacon, lightly toasted slivers of almonds, hazelnuts or walnuts, garlic flavoured croûtons and crisply fried pieces of chestnut.

Stir-fried Sprouts

Serves 4
6-7 sprouts per person
3 cms/1.5 inch piece fresh ginger
1 eating apple
2 tbsp vegetable or sesame oil
Soy sauce

Finely shred the sprouts. Peel and cut the apple into small cubes. Peel and grate the ginger, you will need about one good tbsp.

Heat the oil until really hot. Add the shredded sprouts, apple and grated ginger and stir-fry for two to three minutes. Sprinkle with soy sauce and pepper. Serve.

~

Walnut Tart

Serves 8
Pastry
180g/6oz plain flour
120g/4oz butter
Filling
90g/3oz soft brown sugar
90g/3oz butter

2 eggs
1 lemon
120g/4oz golden syrup
180g/6oz shelled walnuts

Make the pastry and line a 23cm/9inch flan dish.

In the food processor, place the sugar, butter, grated lemon peel and juice, eggs and golden syrup. Whizz until all is well mixed. Add the chopped walnuts and give a quick whizz. Pour into the pastry case. Bake at 180, 350F, Gas 4 for forty-five minutes.

Serve with crème fraîche or vanilla ice-cream.

Orange Salad with wine syrup

Serves 4
6 oranges
30g/1oz Demerara sugar
Wine syrup
275 ml/10fl oz red wine
Small stick of cinnamon
120g/4oz soft brown sugar
1 lemon
60g/2oz toasted shredded almonds

With a sharp knife cut the peel off the oranges. Cut the segments out of the oranges into a pretty bowl. With your hands, squeeze the remaining juice over the segments. Scatter with sugar. Cover and leave to marinate.

In a small pan, put the wine, sugar, cinnamon stick and lemon juice. Boil gently until syrupy. Remove the cinnamon stick and pour into a little jug. Scatter the oranges with the toasted, slivered almonds and serve with the sauce.

There is a wide variety of ingredients in trifle recipes. Fresh and tinned fruit may be used as well as sponge cakes, swiss rolls, macaroons, boudoir biscuits, etc. Jellies and fruit juices are often included and no trifle worth its name is without a good drop of sherry, etc. Normally topped with custard this, too, can be made either using eggs or simply with the help of Mr Bird. Whipped cream is sometimes added on top, decorated, perhaps, with slivered almonds, glacé cherries or angelica.

This is my favourite:

Tipsy Trifle

Serves 8 to 10
6 sponge cakes weighing all together 250g/8 oz
275 ml/10fl oz double cream
60g/2oz ratafia biscuits
Frozen raspberries approx. 120g/4 oz
Raspberry jam
4/5 tbsp sherry or port
30g/1 oz toasted slivered almonds

Custard
275 ml/10fl oz milk
2 egg yolks
30g/1oz sugar
Alternatively use a commercial one

Split the sponge cakes and spread liberally with jam. Stick together then cut them into cubes and scatter into a pretty dish. Pour the sherry or port over allowing it to soak in. Share the raspberries over the top and crumble over the ratafia biscuits.

Make the custard by heating the milk in a small saucepan. Beat the yolks in a bowl with the sugar. Stir in the hot milk, return to the pan and very gently heat until it thickens but don't let it boil. Cool, then pour the custard over the trifle and let it become quite cold. Whip the cream to a soft consistency and spoon over the custard. Decorate with the slivered almonds.

Bananas or tinned fruit may be used instead of the raspberries.

Orange & Lemon Jelly with Macaroons

After a rich dish these jellies are light and refreshing.

Serves 4
275 ml/10fl oz fresh orange juice
275ml/ 10fl oz fresh lemon juice
90g/3oz castor sugar
150 ml/5fl oz double cream, whipped
4 tsp powdered gelatine or one 12g packet

Pour the orange and lemon juice into a bowl, scatter the gelatine on top, add the sugar and place in a pan of hot water, stirring occasionally until all is dissolved.

Remove from the heat and pour into a jug. Then half fill four glasses and refrigerate. When set, spoon in half the whipped cream followed by the remaining jelly.

Refrigerate. Top with the remaining whipped cream.

Serve with macaroons.

Macaroons
120g/4oz ground almonds
120g/4oz castor sugar
1 tsp almond essence
2 egg whites
About 10 skinned or 1 tbsp flaked almonds

In a bowl, lightly whisk the egg whites.Stir in the sugar, ground almonds and essence.Take teaspoonfuls and shape them onto rice paper or silicone paper. Place an almond in the centre of each or scatter flaked almonds. Bake at 180°C, 350°F, Gas 4 for fifteen minutes.

D
E
S
S
E
R
T
S

Festive Mousse

This is rich and irresistible.

Serves 4
3 eggs
120g/4oz soft brown sugar
60g/2oz coarsely grated dark chocolate
90 ml/3fl oz dark rum
3 tsp powdered gelatine
275ml/10fl oz double cream

In a small pan pour in the rum, just warm it then scatter over the gelatine, stirring until it has dissolved. Whisk the egg yolks with half the sugar until thick and pale. Whisk in the rum and gelatine. Whip the cream to a soft consistency and fold into the cooled rum mixture. Whisk the egg whites until stiff, then fold in the remaining sugar. Gently fold it into the rum mixture and spoon into four glasses. When set, scatter with the chocolate.

When the grandchildren are coming for lunch and I ask them what pudding they would like, it is always.....

Golden Syrup Pudding

Serves 6
120g/4oz butter
120g/4oz castor sugar
2 eggs

120g/4oz self-raising flour
3 tbsp golden syrup

Cream the butter and sugar. Add the beaten eggs. Sieve in the flour, folding it in until well mixed. Put the golden syrup in a well buttered basin then spoon in the mixture. Place a piece of greaseproof paper on top and then a piece of foil. Tie it firmly. Place the bowl in a pan of water, bring to the boil and simmer for an hour.
When cooked place a plate on top and invert the pudding. Serve with custard.

Another favourite is Spotted Dick. Instead of golden syrup, use 120g/4oz currants or sultanas.

Bread & Butter Pudding

Bread and butter pudding can be really good. It tends to get ignored, however, possibly because of unhappy childhood memories – or the calorie count!

Serves 4

6 slices of white bread or fruit gâche
   (if using gâche, leave out the fruit)
120g/4oz sultanas or currants
60g/2oz demerara sugar
   (30g/1oz if using gâche)

Nutmeg
3 eggs
30g/1oz butter
275ml/10fl oz milk

Butter the bread or gâche on both sides then cut each slice diagonally. Lay the triangles along a buttered dish, sprinkling the dried fruit in between the slices. Dust with sugar and a grating of nutmeg. Beat the eggs then add the milk. Pour over the bread. Bake at 180°C, 350°F, Gas 4 for twenty minutes.

Lemon Soufflé

This is always a winner. The lemon clears the palate and it is light, just slipping down. It can be served in wine glasses, a cut glass bowl or little cups.

Serves 4

2 eggs
120g/4oz castor sugar
2 lemons
275ml/10fl oz cream
15g/half oz gelatine
150ml/5fl oz water

In a small bowl put the warmed water and sprinkle over the gelatine. While it dissolves, put the egg yolks, sugar, grated lemon rind and juice into a basin. Whisk over hot water until thick and mousse like. Remove from the heat and allow it to cool. Whisk the egg whites and cream separately. When the egg and lemon mixture is quite cold, whisk in the gelatine and then fold in the cream and egg whites. Spoon into glasses or a bowl and refrigerate until needed.

Christmas Pudding

While it may be tempting for the busy housewife to opt for a bought pudding, it is worth taking the trouble to make this most important dessert of the year at home. Christmas Pudding is easy to make and you know exactly what goes in so you can avoid those dreaded E-numbers.

These quantities are sufficient for a 1 litre/2 pt pudding basin.
120g/4oz white breadcrumbs
120g/4oz beef suet or suet of your choice
60g/2oz plain flour
120g/4oz soft brown sugar
Half tsp mixed spice
Quarter tsp grated nutmeg
Half tsp baking powder
Rind and juice of 1 lemon
120g/4oz currants
120g/4oz raisins
60g/2oz sultanas
60g/2oz mixed peel
30g/1oz chopped blanched almonds
1 dessertspoon black treacle
2 eggs
150ml/5fl oz stout
3 tbsp brandy

In a roomy basin put the dried fruit, sugar and almonds, grated lemon peel and juice. Pour over the stout and brandy and leave to soak for several hours, even overnight.

In another roomy basin, put the breadcrumbs and suet. Sieve in the flour, baking powder and spices then add the fruit, beaten eggs and black treacle. When well mixed, pack into a buttered bowl. Cover with two sheets of buttered greaseproof paper and a cloth. Tie all very firmly. Boil for eight hours, adding boiling water if necessary. Store in a cold place. When needed, boil for one hour. Turn out and set alight with a little warmed brandy and carry it in, in style. Serve with brandy butter, custard or ice-cream.

Mincemeat

A recipe from La Société Guernesiaise.

1 kilo/2lbs apples - cored and minced
500g/1lb fresh suet
500g/1lb raisins - minced and stoned
500g/1lb finely powdered sugar
Half tsp mace
2 tsp cinnamon
6 cloves – well pounded
7g/quarter oz salt
The rind of 2 lemons finely cut and the juice of 1
275ml/half pint brandy
275ml/half pint port wine
625g/1.25lbs currants
250g/quarter lb finely chopped candied lemons
Quarter lb finely chopped citron

Mix all the ingredients.

I tried this recipe, adapting it a little and storing the mincemeat in a plastic lidded container.

I thought there was too much alcohol but, amazingly, the fruit absorbed all of it!

Also, I used 500g/1lb candied mixed peel instead of the candied lemons and citron. I added 500g/1lb of sultanas and 120g/4oz glacé cherries.

The Christmas and New Year celebrations are over. We are in January and it is time for the Seville orange and what does that mean? Marmalade. I shall end my journey through the seasons by finishing with two recipes to brighten up the breakfast table.

C
O
N
S
E
R
V
E
S

Seville Orange Marmalade

This, I find is the easiest way of making marmalade:

3 kilos/6lbs Seville oranges   250g/8oz granulated sugar

Wash the oranges and place in a large saucepan. Cover with water, bring to boiling point and simmer for about forty-five minutes until easily pierced. Remove the oranges with a slotted spoon and let them cool. When cool enough to handle, cut in half and with a spoon, remove the pith and flesh and put it in a muslin bag or cloth spread over a colander placed over a bowl. Slice the peel and return to the saucepan. Heat the contents and when boiling stir in the sugar, stirring until it is dissolved. Tie the bag or cloth containing the flesh and put it in the saucepan. Once boiling point is reached again, boil for about thirty minutes. Spoon a little on a saucer and test for setting. Pot in the usual way.

Lemon Curd

This is quick and easy to make and the curd can be simply potted, spooned into a pastry case to make a delicious lemon tart or, by covering with whipped up egg whites, transformed into lemon meringue pie. Potted lemon curd should always be kept in the fridge.

   3 large eggs
   3 lemons
   90g/3oz butter
   250g/8oz granulated sugar

Whisk the eggs and place in a double saucepan or bowl that fits over a pan of water. Bring to a rolling boil. Add the finely grated peel and juice of the lemons. Add the butter and sugar and stir until melted. Continue to simmer until thick – about thirty minutes – stirring occasionally. Pot in the usual way.

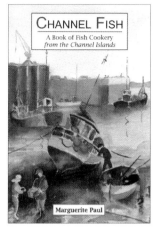

Also by Marguerite Paul ~

CHANNEL FISH: *A Book of Fish Cookery from the Channel Islands*

This book is the fruit of a lifetime's passion for cooking and eating fish. Marguerite Paul is Guernsey born and bred, though she has lived much of her life overseas – in North Africa, the Middle East, India and the Far East.

Her fishy preoccupations began in childhood expeditions to the beaches and rock pools around the coast of her native island, where she collected and brought home some of the wealth of wild food which was freely available. Her interest in fish cookery developed during her travels in foreign parts, when she adapted her recipes to include more exotic ingredients and experimented with various local dishes.

Fish, crustaceans, molluscs and cephalopods are included here – some 50 species in all – for which are presented around 130 recipes, many very simple for everyday eating, others more elaborate but ideal for that special occasion.

Marguerite's recipes are prefaced with advice on the occasionally off-putting business of preparing fish for cooking, and rounded off with notes on how to concoct a range of lipsmacking stocks, sauces and dips.

Tune in to CHANNEL FISH and prepare to enjoy a fishy feast!

224 pages   Price £11.95

Some other Seaflower Books ~

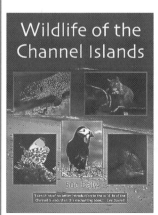

Complete list of Seaflower Books, 2012:

BLAME THE BADGER by Mike Stentiford OBE	£6.95
CHANNEL FISH by Marguerite Paul	£11.95
EXOTIC GARDEN PLANTS INTHE CHANNEL ISLANDS by Janine Le Pivert	£9.95
A FARMER'S VACATION IN 1873 by George E Waring	£5.00
GUERNSEY COUNTRY DIARY by Nigel Jee	£4.95
ISLAND DESTINY by Richard Le Tissier	£6.95
ISLAND KITCHEN by Marguerite Paul	£11.95
JERSEY HORSES FROM THE PAST by John Jean	£4.95
JERSEY IN LONDON by Brian Ahier Read	£6.95
JERSEY JAUNTS by John Le Dain	£5.95
THE JERSEY LILY by Sonia Hillsdon	£5.95
JERSEY: NOT QUITE BRITISH by David Le Feuvre	£6.95
JERSEY OCCUPATION DIARY by Nan Le Ruez	£9.95
JERSEY OCCUPATION REMEMBERED by Sonia Hillsdon	£5.95
JERSEY RAMBLES by John Le Dain	£6.95
JERSEY WAR WALKS by Ian Ronayne	£7.95
JERSEY WEATHER AND TIDES by Peter Manton	£5.95
JERSEY WITCHES, GHOSTS & TRADITIONS by by Sonia Hillsdon	£6.95
JOHN SKINNER'S VISIT TO THE CHANNEL ISLANDS: August 1827	£2.50
JOURNEY ACROSS JERSEY by Robin Pittman	£5.95
JOURNEY ROUND JERSEY by Robin Pittman	£7.95
JOURNEY ROUND ST HELIER by Robin Pittman	£7.95
LES MINQUIERS by Jeremy Mallinson	£7.95
LIFE ON SARK by Jennifer Cochrane	£5.95
LOW WATER FISHING by David Le Maistre	£6.95
MINED WHERE YOU WALK by Richard Le Tissier	£6.95
THE POOR SHALL INHERIT Daff Noel	£6.95
PRISON WITHOUT BARS by Frank Keiller	£6.95
WILD ISLAND by Peter Double	£7.95
WILDLIFE OF THE CHANNEL ISLANDS by Sue Daly	£14.95

Please visit our website for more details: **www.ex-librisbooks.co.uk**
SEAFLOWER BOOKS may be ordered through our website using Paypal
We send books post-free within the UK and Channel Islands
SEAFLOWER BOOKS are also available via your local bookshop or from Amazon.com

SEAFLOWER BOOKS

11 Regents Place, Bradford on Avon, Wiltshire, BA15 1ED
Tel/Fax 01225 865191   e-mail: roger.jones@ex-librisbooks.co.uk
www.ex-librisbooks.co.uk